The Best of the Rest

DOWNSIZING FOR
BOOMERS AND SENIORS

Nancy

Thank you for what
you've done for me

Enjoy !!

Judy Robinson

March 4, 2010

The Best of the Rest is dedicated to
our sons, Mike and Andrew,
their wives, Sue and Melissa,
our daughter, Sue, her husband, Rich,
and our nine wonderful grandchildren.

The Best
OF
The Rest

DOWNSIZING FOR
BOOMERS AND SENIORS

Doug and Judy Robinson

GSPH

GENERAL STORE PUBLISHING HOUSE
499 O'Brien Road, Box 415
Renfrew, Ontario, Canada K7V 4A6
Telephone 1.613.432.7697 or 1.800.465.6072
www.gsph.com

ISBN 978-1-897508-68-8

Illustrations: Gary Frederick
Design, formatting: Magdalene Carson / New Leaf Publication Design
Printed by Custom Printers of Renfrew Ltd., Renfrew, Ontario
Printed and bound in Canada

Library and Archives Canada Cataloguing in Publication

Robinson, Doug, 1937-
    The best of the rest : downsizing for boomers and seniors / Doug
Robinson, Judy Robinson.

ISBN 978-1-897508-68-8

    1. Older people--Housing. 2. Moving, Household. I. Robinson,
Judy, 1942- II. Title.

HD7287.9.R63 2010   363.5'946   C2010-900604-6

Contents

Acknowledgments

Thanks to Anna Christina Robinson, a very giving and caring
lady, whom we first downsized.
Little did we know that it would become a second career.

Thanks to Jack Johannsen, Judy's dad,
who gave her the ability to dream and persevere.

Thanks to Kent Browne, whose request for a "favor"
sent us on this wonderful journey.

Thanks to Charles Darwin Snelling, for whose interest and
encouragement we are grateful.

Thanks to Paul Kitchen, sports historian and author
extraordinaire, whose sage advice and fine example
was most helpful and inspiring,

Thanks to Jane Karchmar, our editor.
To work with Jane has been a delight!

Thanks to Tim Gordon, our publisher, for keeping us on track.

And last but not least, thanks to our numerous friends, the
thousands of boomers and seniors we've guided and assisted
with the downsizing process, and the many veterans we've had
the pleasure of meeting and working with . . . our heroes.

Introduction

IT WAS RAINY, WINDY, AND COLD that late fall day in 1996. A ninety-year-old gentleman had gone into a retirement residence leaving his older home jammed full of "stuff." A real estate friend, who knew we had a trailer, asked if we would empty the house so he could sell it. There we were, two retired teachers, throwing forty years of hoarded "treasures"—broken light fixtures, string, tinfoil, newspapers—over the wall at the local landfill.

In the midst of this, the light came on: the realization that there must be many seniors out there who need to move but have no idea how to "get out from under" all those years of accumulated possessions.

We soon realized that seniors also needed specialized help with moving and getting resettled, and we made it our goal to do it as stress-free as possible.

Imagine that! An idea that would forever change our lives and bring peace of mind to so many seniors, boomers, and their families was born at the CITY DUMP!

Looking back over the years, it became clear that a wide variety of life experiences had prepared us for our "second career." The ensuing years have given us additional knowledge and experience to guide our clients through the entire downsizing process gently, supportively, and compassionately.

We've been asked to share our expertise through radio talk shows, seminars, and network and local television, as well as consulting for local, national, and international publications. All of this has allowed us to help countless unseen numbers of boomers, seniors, and their families.

We hope that *Downsizing for Boomers and Seniors*, the result of our accumulated knowledge and experience, will enlighten and guide you through the downsizing process as well as help you make better and more informed decisions along the way.

You may wish to read only those chapters that address your particular concerns. There are a few repetitions we felt were necessary for this reason.

Please remember that this is not legal advice—this book is to help you think, organize your thoughts, and ask questions before you make any decisions or commitments. Our purpose here and throughout the book is to help you to make your own informed decisions.

CHAPTER 1

Is It Time to Move?

TO MOVE OR NOT TO MOVE?

This is a question many people are facing as they retire and grow older. Can they afford to stay in their home? Should they buy something smaller or newer? Should they rent an apartment or buy a condo? Should they choose a community that will have support services available if and when they might need them or is a secluded spot in the country more to their liking? It's wise to explore all options and plan ahead.

Several years ago, a new retirement residence opened, and friends of ours, a couple in their seventies, went to see it. Both were in good health, but they decided if they ever had to move,

this would be their choice. They put their names on a waiting list "just in case" and continued living very active lives.

One winter while holidaying down south, the wife was rushed to a hospital, air-ambulanced back, and told she could not return to her home. The husband phoned the residence to see if they had a two-bedroom suite and was told that all they had were two small rooms beside each other. We suggested that they take the two rooms and use one as a bedroom and the other as a living room/office until a two-bedroom suite became available. They sold their five-bedroom home, put some furniture in storage, and began settling in. Several months later, they did move into their two-bedroom suite. Advanced planning and some flexibility had served them well! It is much better to plan ahead and decide what will work for you as you grow older.

For boomers, the motivation for moving is usually optional, dictated by the end of a career and the beginning of a new adventure, or fulfilling a dream they have nurtured for years. Nevertheless, some sons and daughters will selfishly have misgivings about the decisions their parents are making.

Boomers will have a much easier time deciding what to do for themselves than guiding an elderly relative through the process. Sometimes a child feels a parent should move, when actually aging in place might be a wiser choice. Other times, a senior *should* move, and the family is unable to see the need. It is important to know if a loved one should move or if he/she can still have some quality time in his/her own home with the aid of medications and a support system of caring people and needed services. A geriatric assessment can help narrow down the options.

GENERAL QUESTIONS

Look at the following list and identify the items that are relevant to you or your loved one.

- Is staying in your home becoming a financial strain?
- Is cash flow needed to improve the quality of life?
- Is housekeeping becoming more of a struggle?
- Is home maintenance now a nuisance or becoming increasingly unmanageable?

- Is yard work becoming a chore?
- Does the house need major repairs?
- Is the house too big?
- Are stairs getting more difficult?
- Has the neighborhood changed and is security now a concern?
- Is the location no longer convenient?
- Do you want a new lifestyle?
- Is there a desire to travel more?
- Is there a dream you want to fulfill while you still can?
- Have the children left home or are they planning to move out?
- Is there a "freeloader" living in the house, and your moving is the only way out?
- Has downsizing or moving already been considered?

QUESTIONS FOR ELDERS

- Have there been several falls?
- Is the bathroom becoming difficult to use or a safety concern?
- Is the thought of a stroke or a fall (and being alone) frightening?
- Is Parkinson's disease, arthritis, emphysema, multiple sclerosis, macular degeneration, diabetes, dementia, or the effects from a heart attack or stroke getting much worse?
- Is help needed with dressing and bathing?
- Is someone needed to monitor medications?
- Is caring for a spouse becoming overwhelming?
- Is worry about needing help and not getting it becoming more frequent?
- Is loneliness increasing?
- Is your circle of friends shrinking?
- Is television your only social life?
- Has your doctor said you need to move?

How many of these are pertinent to your situation? A significant number can confirm what you have already been thinking or alleviate some of the guilt feelings about parents that the family members may be experiencing. A better quality of life should always be the goal.

WHAT ARE THE BENEFITS OF A MOVE?

General

- No stairs
- Less responsibility
- Better security
- Better location
- More freedom to travel
- Less maintenance
- Freeing up capital from a house
- Companionship
- Closer to family

Elders

- Activities
- Housekeeping
- Nursing care
- Nutritious meals
- Supervision of medications
- Assistance with daily living
- Other (list any others you can think of)

WHAT WOULD STAY THE SAME IF THE RELOCATION WERE IN THE SAME AREA?

- Friends
- Doctor
- Hairdresser
- Bank
- Independence
- Times with family
- Place of worship
- Phone number
- Possession of car
- Holidays
- Memberships in service clubs
- Participation in social groups
- Other (list any others)

WHAT COULD BE LOST?

- Familiar surroundings
- Some space
- Some privacy
- Some possessions
- Friendships
- Other (list any others)

CONCERNS THAT CAN PRECIPITATE A MOVE

Health problems

They can be sudden, such as an incapacitating fall (a broken hip is the most common), a heart attack, or a stroke; these are often unexpected. Or one could develop conditions over time such as multiple sclerosis, Parkinson's disease, arthritis, diabetes, dementia, macular degeneration, Alzheimer's,[1] etc.

Too much responsibility

Having to look after a home, pay the bills, shop, and cook can become overwhelming. A man recently stated that he needed to get these things "looked after" so he could have the time to do the things he really wanted to do.

Loneliness

Even if you visit your parent every day, he or she can still be left alone much of the day. Sometimes older people will sit alone in the dark with absolutely no mental stimulation.

Nutrition

We saw Doug's mom nearly every day. Strange as it may seem, I don't think we realized at first how poorly she was eating. Any talk about lamb chops for supper and eggs for breakfast was just that—talk. Not that she couldn't afford it—she just didn't eat! While cleaning out her house, we discovered enough canned goods to stock a food bank. We often see this; many people don't like eating alone.

Loss of driver's license

This has precipitated many senior moves.

LOOKING AHEAD

Some residences in our city have a five-to-ten-year waiting list. At one seniors' apartment complex, forty people have given a $1,000 deposit just to be on the waiting list. Certain condos are in great demand. As baby boomers age, excellent apartments, condos, and residences in a reasonable price range will become scarcer. Boomers, how do you want to spend your golden years?

Typically, we get emergency calls where a senior is suddenly being discharged from a hospital, and essential belongings need to be moved to a retirement facility within forty-eight hours or less. Often the place the ailing senior is moving to is determined

---

1　See the chapter on Alzheimer's.

by someone who is unfamiliar with their personal needs and aspirations. Due to limited time to do the research and make a choice, the place the elder "lands in" may not be his/her second, fifth, or even twentieth choice.

Family members, social workers, and lawyers often have this decision-making responsibility when a person is hospitalized and the doctor has said, "Going home is not an option." Decisions are made under great duress because frequently the people involved have never envisioned being in such a situation and have given no thought as to what they might do should this occur.

Children of seniors need to begin thinking about a possible move for their parents down the road. Even if a move doesn't seem probable, find out what is available, what services are provided, and what commitments they're willing to make. Check them out yourself. If the time to move suddenly arrives, you will be somewhat prepared to discuss the topic with your family. Few of us are comfortable discussing moving, the loss of a driver's license, or the possible death or declining health of a parent — but at times it is necessary.

CHAPTER 2

Aging in Place

"AGING IN PLACE" is growing older in your own home or in another residence that is more adaptable to future needs.

As retirement was approaching, we started looking for a smaller house and a different lifestyle. We actually looked for ten years but bought our new home in ten minutes! Doug wanted a farm or waterfront home with some property and "something to do." Judy wanted a city phone number, the ability to see people from the window, shopping nearby, and a dining area that would hold the whole family. Everything on the same level was a priority!

We chose a 960-square-foot converted cottage on a river close to town. There is boating, swimming, and fishing in the summer and many winter activities. The view is fabulous, yet from the kitchen window I can see people walking, jogging, biking, and rollerblading. We have a city phone number, and ten minutes away there is a store with fresh meat, home baking, fresh flowers, and wine. We can even call the store and order a medium-sized roast cooked to order to be picked up at a set time. Few places have this customized service! And yes, we have had many

family dinners. Several friends have also bought in our area when they saw how much we enjoyed our new lifestyle.

AGING IN PLACE IN YOUR OWN HOME

Most seniors desire to live in their homes as long as possible (90 percent, according to AARP[2]). Few people have actually done the research to know if it's right for them or even how to make it happen. Will your home actually work for you as you get older? Are there health concerns that can't be ignored and could in fact scuttle the whole idea?

When homes are "senior-friendly" and enough support services are put in place, seniors can often stay comfortably and safely in their own residences. Unfortunately, some people don't have the finances to own their home and also pay for necessary services. Others are too proud to accept help even if it is available.

PRIMARY CONCERNS

- Is it still a good, safe location? (Near services, family or friends)
- Can it be adapted easily and reasonably to meet your needs?
- If your house is two storeys, how long will those aging legs manage the stairs? Or can the stairwell accommodate an electric chair lift?
- Can the house accommodate minor or major renovations if necessary?
- Is your house structurally sound? Contact a reputable building inspector and get a report on the overall condition of your dwelling. You want to know if there will be any major surprises that could become a financial burden down the road. Some of these might include:

Roof	Asbestos
Foundation	Mold
Windows	Termites
Heating	Well (if there is one)
Cooling	Septic system (if you live in a
Wiring	rural area)
Plumbing	

---

2   American Association of Retired Persons.

· Could the living room, bedroom, bathroom, kitchen, and laundry be on one level? Some people build an addition with a bedroom and ensuite bath. Others use the family room or dining room as a bedroom and add a bathroom on the ground level. Many have a stackable washer and dryer installed in the kitchen or bathroom.

OPTIONAL RENOVATIONS FOR A SENIOR-FRIENDLY HOME

Bathroom

Most bathrooms in older homes need to be adapted to meet the special needs of seniors. Many washroom doors are too narrow to accommodate a walker or wheelchair. Also if the bathroom is small, a fall against the door could block rescuers. A pocket door that slides into the wall is a good preventative measure. Another option is a quality folding door. Consider:

· A shower or walk-in tub
· Arthritic-friendly taps with a heat regulator
· Professionally installed grab bars
· Accessible drawers for storage
· Proper lighting
· Decora light switches[3]
· Phone, intercom, or emergency button
· A floor surface that is senior-friendly and easy to maintain[4]
· Other ideas

Kitchen

· A walker- or wheelchair-friendly entrance; if a walker or wheelchair is used in the house, two doorways for the kitchen would be wise
· Counters and cupboards adjusted to convenient heights
· D-shaped handles rather than knobs
· Pivoting or rotating shelves in corner cabinets

---

3 Decora light switches are large toggle switches that are easier for older people to use. Some of them produce a dim light that is easy to see in the dark.
4 For example, a soft linoleum; obviously nothing slippery—no throw rugs, etc.

- Countertops with rounded edges
- Sink adjusted to a convenient height
- Space made under the sink so you can sit and work
- Faucet installed with a single lever to control flow and temperature
- Enough electrical outlets in convenient locations
- Excellent lighting
- Decora light switches
- A vertical cupboard or pantry
- A stove with accessible knobs
- A heat-proof surface beside the stove
- Microwave at a convenient height
- A floor surface that is senior-friendly and easy to maintain
- Other ideas

Front door

Some people are installing automatic garage door openers on the front doors. As well, you can install an intercom or TV monitor so that you can hear or see visitors before the door is opened. Other considerations:

- At least thirty-two inches wide
- Lever door handles
- Well-lit area
- A keyless locking system
- Other ideas

Exterior ramp

- A professionally built ramp that is not too steep
- A landing at the bottom and top of the ramp (and perhaps halfway up)
- A surface that is not slippery when wet
- Guard rails to prevent accidents
- Handrails on both sides of the ramp

Look at your home carefully. Can you adapt it to meet your needs or should you consider buying something that is more suitable or flexible — possibly in the same area?

ADDITIONAL CONSIDERATIONS
TO HELP KEEP INDEPENDENCE

- A simple security system to give extra safety and added peace of mind
- A "roomer" (possibly an older professional man or woman) to provide some companionship and help one feel more secure, especially at night
- A "buddy system," where someone calls at certain times to make certain one is okay
- Someone hired to come daily and provide meals, light housework, reminders for medication, and perhaps needed companionship.
- TELECARE — a growing telecommunications field that allows people to live independently[5]
- A lifeline or specialized phone service to provide immediate help if needed
- A video conferencing system that allows the senior to see and talk with family members
- A telephone service available in some areas to monitor eating habits, medications taken, blood pressure, glucose levels, moods, and whether the senior has had any visitors (this service is becoming popular in many places. Some services also keep a child informed as to how a parent is doing each day.)
- Specialized sensors that keep track of running water, people wandering at unusual times, appliances that have been left on, etc. They have auditory reminders set up with the familiar voice of someone the person trusts, saying, "Turn off the water" . . . "Turn off the stove" . . . etc.

Some systems are also set up to send a text message to a relative if a sensor is set off.

---

5   A growing number of companies are monitoring seniors' everyday lives. It is new technology and not available everywhere. This technology enables seniors to get immediate help in case of a fall, stroke, or heart attack. Some systems in England (in their infancy here) actually send a report covering whether a senior has taken his/her medication, eaten, had visitors, even how he/she is feeling that day. If there is a problem, help can be sent to the senior and an electronic report can be quickly sent to a caregiver or child, even in another city.

PREVENTING FALLS

A major concern for seniors is falling: 1.8 million elderly people went to hospitals in the United States in a single year because of falls. Many did not recover. A large percentage of our emergency calls are for people who can't return to their homes because of falls and must enter some type of care facility, often on short notice.

Many accidents are preventable. It is important to make a senior's environment as safe as possible. Some easy first steps:

- Get rid of clutter.
- Remove scatter rugs.
- Limit footstools.
- Install handrails where needed.
- Ensure dust ruffles aren't too long.
- If needed, shorten bathrobes. (A friend's mom tripped on her nightie. She had shrunk with osteoporosis, and some of her clothing had become a hazard due to their excessive length.)
- Remove ladders if necessary. (Judy found her elderly grandmother up on a ladder painting. She asked to "borrow" the ladder and kept "forgetting" to return it!)
- Improve lighting in the home. We've seen many seniors using 40-watt bulbs where 100 watts are necessary. (At times we found Doug's mom sitting in a dark room . . . she was saving electricity!)
- Have a pharmacist check all medications to see if any of them could cause dizziness or fatigue. All outdated medications should be discarded as well.
- Get vision checked. Different glasses for different activities may be required.
- Encourage seniors to remain active. Exercise will improve balance and strength. Unfortunately, fear of a fall can actually precipitate one by their refusal to exercise.

IDENTIFYING NEEDED SERVICES AND THEIR AVAILABILITY

If you or a loved one wants to age in place and are willing to accept help, see what services are needed, whether they are available in your area, and what the costs are.

See if there are subsidies or financing available to defray some of the cost. In some locations, people with disabilities are provided with government-funded care-giving. In some countries, money is available to help veterans stay in their own homes. A motion chair, stair lift, or specialized bed also could be provided. Use this list to help estimate your expenses.

Services needed:

Cost:

Assistance available:

- Shopping
- Meals prepared in the home
- Prepared meals delivered
- Laundry
- Bathing
- Paying bills
- Nursing care
- Assistance with housework
- Interior maintenance
- Exterior maintenance
- A driver for doctor appointments
- An in-home hair care service
- An in-home foot-care service
- Other (list)

If children are part of the equation, they might be willing to make a financial or time commitment to help bring it all together. Judy set aside Thursday mornings to take Doug's parents grocery shopping. Although it would have been easier for us to pick up the groceries, it was important for their physical and mental well being to get them out of the house.

You may remember one of Lynn Johnston's cartoons where an elderly lady leaves the dentist's office and says, "I used to hate going to the dentist but now it is an OUTING!"

Finally, in all this, keep in mind that in many instances, major problems with aging are loneliness and poor nutrition. If someone is with them two hours a day, there are still twenty-two hours of being alone. Also, many people don't like eating alone, and even if food is available you can't guarantee it will be eaten.

SHARING A HOME

Many seniors are sharing their homes with family members. Sometimes it works, sometimes it doesn't. Marriages are breaking up and a child and the grandchildren move back home. Adult children are losing their jobs and returning to the security of the home they grew up in. Grandchildren "move in" with grandma to attend college or start their first job. Keep in mind that the financial strain on the senior can be overwhelming when there is no financial help from the "boarder."

If possible, establish guidelines before anyone moves in.

· How long may they stay?
· How are they expected to contribute? (finances, chores)
· Is there a "quiet hour"?
· May friends sleep over?

CAUTION: We have seen seniors sign over their homes to a child, believing that he or she could live with the child and be looked after in their own home forever. What if a child ends up with major health problems or gets into debt and the house has to be sold? What happens if the daughter's marriage breaks up and the ex wants 50 percent of the value of his "wife's home"? Things don't always go as planned. Problems such as jealousy on the part of other children can surface. Siblings can be very upset if they feel their inheritance is threatened or if they think their parent is being taken advantage of.

Can a daughter lift a heavy parent if necessary? Is it safe for the parent to be left alone even for a few minutes if he/she has advanced dementia? Again, think carefully before you make a commitment or encourage a sibling to make one. *Talk with a lawyer about the pitfalls of the arrangement.*

SENIORS' DAY-CARE

Parents are living longer, and many offspring have some of the responsibility for their care.

In some areas, seniors' day-care centers are opening. These help seniors to remain in their homes and help alleviate some of the stress adult children feel trying to balance work and family obligations. In fact, some businesses are experimenting with providing this service for parents of their employees to help alleviate stress for their staff. Existing retirement homes are also looking at providing this service. They already have fitness programs, activities, and meals in place. If the space is available to accommodate the extra seniors during the daytime, only transportation needs to be provided. There is a cost for this service and it varies from place to place. As our population ages, this need will increase.

NEIGHBORHOOD-BASED STRATEGIES

Some seniors are members of registered nonprofit organizations that provide necessary services that enable them to remain in their homes. These organizations have lined up providers of transportation, home repair, food services, companionship, daily security check-ins, and other services to meet the needs of their members in their homes. There is an annual fee, and extra services — such as a home health aide — are available for additional fees. Although these growing neighborhood-based communities are enabling seniors to live independently in their own homes, they are not the answer for those with complicated medical needs. If staying in the home is not an option, then another form of independent living can be considered.

CHAPTER 3

Downsizing — Lots of Choices for Boomers or Seniors

YEARS AGO, MANY PEOPLE died at an earlier age. Few couples lived long enough to celebrate their fiftieth wedding anniversary. Now some are celebrating their sixty-fifth. Many are still driving, traveling, and living active lives. In the past, most families lived in the same community all their lives and the surviving parent or parents would often live with their extended family. If they left, they were usually going to a nursing home to die! Nowadays, with families dispersing in all directions and many women in the work force, elderly parents have a need for other alternatives outside the traditional family unit. This growing demand has created a wide range of living accommodations. Seniors can actually make choices that *improve* their quality of life.

In the twenty-first century, downsizing can take on many forms. Some seniors and a lot of boomers will choose both a new lifestyle and a change of address. Others will do what they can to remain in their own homes.

The most common form of downsizing is *spatial,* in which people find smaller accommodations when their large home is no longer needed or too much to look after. Unfortunately, this can result in some downsizing of privacy as well.

Financial downsizing is cutting down on your household expenses. This can include the amount of money that is invested in your residence, taxes, fixed monthly costs, maintenance, repairs, and services that may be needed. This usually involves moving to less expensive accommodations.

Some people choose to downsize in space, yet upsize financially. A new adult lifestyle bungalow can cost more than the older, more spacious two-storey home a couple currently lives in.

SPATIAL OPTIONS

· A bungalow
· A condo
· An apartment
· A mobile home
· A life lease
· Sharing a home or apartment with family members or a close friend
· An apartment or a room in a family member's home
· An apartment in the senior's home (some seniors will choose to live in the apartment, usually on the ground floor, while others will rent out the apartment for the income)
· A roomer in the house to provide income and company (we have seen a young adult grandchild live with a grandparent)
· An independent bungalow on a family member's property
· A granny suite
· A retirement residence
· A nursing home
· Renting a room (sometimes with specialized care) in a private home
· A group home (a private bedroom, shared kitchen, living room)
· Assisted living
· A continuing care retirement community

Some people are downsizing to a small apartment in town and purchasing their "dream home" in the country. Others opt for a winter home down south.

ADDITIONAL OPTIONS TO FULFILL DREAMS

- A cabin in the mountains
- A house on the water
- A motor home
- A live-aboard boat
- A home or apartment in another country or a warmer climate

Many of these examples are covered in later chapters.

THOUGHTS TO CONSIDER WHEN DOWNSIZING

- Is it a priority to be close to family and friends? (Is it easy for people to visit on a regular basis?)
- Is staying in a familiar neighborhood a preference?
- Is the neighborhood in decline?
- If looking at a new area, is it a safe community?
- Is walking in the area an option? (Is it too busy, are there frequent crimes or other neighborhood issues?)
- How safe is the building being considered?
- Is twenty-four-hour security or a gated community important?
- Is a quiet lifestyle desirable?
- Is living downtown more attractive?
- Is parking available?
- Will it be easy to park?
- Will it be easy for visitors to park?
- Are the nearby streets "friendly" for senior drivers?
- Is it close to public transportation?
- Is there a concern about stairs?
- Is there a concern about elevators?
- Is there a pharmacy nearby? (Does it take phone orders? Does it make deliveries?)
- Is it close to doctors, dentists? (Are they taking new patients?)
- Is it close to a hospital or medical clinic?
- Is there a grocery store in the area? (Do they make deliveries?)
- Are services such as banks, libraries, and dry cleaners within walking distance?

- Is there a suitable place of worship nearby?
- Are there restaurants in the area? (Do they deliver?)
- Is there a problem having people living beside or above? (Adult-lifestyle bungalows can be fishbowls, depending on their design.)
- Is it a good location that will appreciate or hold its value if you are buying?
- If there is empty land nearby, what will it be used for?

Few places will meet all expectations, so you will have to decide which comes closest to satisfying most of your priorities.

For some individuals, this can be the hardest move they have ever made. They have spent a lifetime collecting things and suddenly they can keep only a fraction of their possessions. It's not only eighty- or ninety-year-olds. We have seen several sixty-year-olds sell or store possessions and take off down the road for several years. Husbands can find the adventure exciting, while wives, on the other hand, can find such a change emotional and exhausting, especially when friends, family, and grandchildren are left behind.

People usually find the unknown intimidating. Individuals don't like change, especially seniors who are more set in their ways. There is something very comforting about keeping the status quo even if the situation isn't the best. A move can be logical but the thought of it can be psychologically daunting.

We have found that although many seniors don't want to move, they "know" they should and the thoughts of it are overwhelming. It's fatiguing to think you *should* do *something* but really have no idea what to do, let alone where to begin.

We went to see a mother and her daughter. Mom had had several falls in two months. The daughter was determined that her mom would move. The mother refused! We addressed the fact that she did not want to move. Judy then put her hand near her own heart, looked at the mom, and said, "Right in here you know it's time to move." The mother acknowledged that it was time, and we planned her move. Mom made the decision. She had determined that no one was going to tell her what to do, even if it was what she needed to do.

EXAMPLES OF FINANCIAL DOWNSIZING

Many of our eighty-year-old clients are selling their homes and buying less expensive condos. Some of our eighty-five-year-olds have had extensive renovations done to their condos and were still ahead financially. (The work was done before they moved in.) They had an investment, but still had some cash flow to pay for extra help and services. Some people have moved from a two-bedroom apartment or a two-bedroom suite in a retirement residence to a one-bedroom unit to free up cash to pay for needed help or travel.

Several years ago, our son rented a one-bedroom apartment for $600 a month. He found it very expensive, so he rented a two-bedroom apartment for $700 and shared it with a friend. His savings were $250 a month.

Many times we have seen a senior share a two-bedroom apartment with a sister, a brother, a friend, or a cousin. Or they might share a two-bedroom unit in a retirement residence. Where possible, we encourage them to get a unit with two bathrooms; and to try living together before they make it a permanent situation.

A couple invited her parents to live with them. Within a short time, they knew that they had made an emotional decision and not a workable one.

A widow, after months of loneliness, asked a close friend to share her home. They had enjoyed holidays together but discovered that constant contact soon took its toll on their friendship.

A client who was a devoted wife sold all her possessions except for her clothes and a sentimental pen, to share a room in a nursing home with her husband. When he died, she was able to move but all her treasured belongings were gone. (A secure storage facility would have been a useful option.)

On the other hand, one lady with health concerns moved into a single room in a retirement residence. Hoping her health would improve, she put enough of her belongings into storage to furnish a one-bedroom condo or apartment. The cost was worth it because it not only left room for optimism, but also gave her peace of mind.

When someone is considering a move, the most important decision he or she can make is location, location, location! We have seen many clients commit to moving thousands of miles away to enjoy a warmer climate or proximity to relatives only to discover they have left behind irreplaceable relationships and support systems built up over many years. Keep in mind that it is not as difficult to adjust to a move if there is a support system in place such as friends, family, health care, etc. It is also easier to adapt to a new community if you're younger, healthy, active, and have a partner.

A geriatric social worker recently said the worst mistake many people make when they are elderly is to move far from all their familiar surroundings. On the other hand, if a parent has advanced dementia or major health problems, it can be wise to have them move closer to a child who can check on them and provide for their needs.

CAUTION! Relatives may be enthusiastic about a parent moving closer, but have they really thought about how big a time commitment is necessary? Moving a parent to a new location, leaving familiar relationships behind, then only seeing them for Sunday dinners is not enough.

Whatever the choice, look at a trial run, if feasible, before "dynamiting all bridges" — selling most possessions, or committing to living with someone, only to discover it was a big mistake.

FACTORS TO CONSIDER BEFORE MOVING A PARENT NEAR YOU

- Are you working full time?
- What level of commitment are you willing to make to your parent? (Sunday dinners . . .)
- Is your parent good at making new friends? (Men usually have a harder time adjusting.)
- Does your parent like his/her own company?
- Can mom (or dad) adjust to a new doctor or hairdresser?
- Is your parent a complainer or does he/she try to make the best of everything?
- Is this an opportunity for a grandparent to spend quality time with grandchildren?
- Is the senior good at trying new things?
- What will you do about holidays?
- How does your partner feel about your commitment?

Remember, your parents will be in a strange city and will know no one except you and your family. Suggest that they come for a month. Most retirement residences have respite rooms or furnished suites that can be rented for a short time. All your loved one needs to bring is some clothing and personal items. This gives everyone a chance to see if it will work or not. Often we've seen seniors who sell everything and move to be near children and grandchildren end up being very lonely and unhappy. We have seen many return to their roots quite bitter about the experience they have had. Occasionally we see amazing moves where a parent has made an excellent transition and now has quality time with grandchildren they hardly knew before.

An elderly couple, after meeting and "joining forces" in a retirement residence, were moving out to an apartment in a seniors' building. They had been out shopping like a young engaged couple in love. As we moved their belongings, they were like prisoners breaking out of jail. They realized that with each other they weren't as dependent on supportive care as they had thought.

Many times a year, we get calls from people who have changed their minds and want to return to their home. If it hasn't sold, and they are healthy enough, they can. We moved a lady in her nineties to a retirement suite, and a few days later, she phoned to say, "I'm going home!"

We discreetly phoned her son and said, "We've been talking with your mom."

He said, "She wants to go home. Move her as soon as you can."

We have also heard of many people who have bought a small condominium downtown and lasted only a short while. Some didn't like the noise, the crime, or the elevators. Others missed a backyard or the space they had. We have also heard of people moving to the country for a time. Some didn't like the isolation. Others found that friends didn't want to drive to visit them. Some missed shopping and entertainment. Still others wanted to be closer to doctors and hospitals.

If your choices don't work out, can you still change your mind? With all decisions, "Look before you leap!"

CHAPTER 4

Adult Bungalow, Condo, Apartment, or More Adventurous Downsizing

FRIENDS WERE SO HAPPY to be buying a brand-new adult bungalow. There were health problems and it was necessary to sell their large home in the country. Until they actually moved, they didn't realize what an adjustment it would be to live so close to so many other people. There were no trees, and fences were not permitted. Suddenly even a cup of coffee sipped outside could be observed by a multitude of neighbors. They considered moving but instead called in a landscape designer, who came up with helpful solutions to give them some privacy. They now enjoy their neighbors and no longer feel they are "living in a fishbowl."

A woman chose her adult lifestyle condo because of the beautiful view of tranquil fields beside her. Unfortunately, developers built a strip mall there, and now her view is a line of service

doors. Delivery trucks frequently arrive during the middle of the night and disturb her sleep.

Sometimes you can rectify a wrong decision. Occasionally you may need to move again!

Many seniors move into adult bungalows, condos, and apartments. Some are choosing homes in the mountains or a year-round place on the water. Often they build or renovate when necessary. The more adventurous ones are selling everything and buying large motor homes, fifth wheel trailers, or live-aboard boats. With cell phones, computers, and wireless Internet, they can stay in touch daily with loved ones and monitor investments, news events, and so on. They are downsizing in many different ways but their goal is the same: a better quality of life!

Adult bungalows, condos, and apartments are popping up everywhere from city centers to outlying areas where shopping and services can be quite limited. Seniors should be cautious about choosing something that is too isolated. If they lose their driver's license, it will force them to rely on others, especially if there is no public transit. Also, a remote location could be a problem when reselling. And we have heard of many seniors building their dream home or cottage in the country only to discover that their friends wouldn't drive "that far" to visit.

Conversely, caution should be used before buying or renting a small, downtown unit. We know several fifty-year-olds who sold their suburban home and purchased small, expensive condos in town centers. They wanted to be near work, restaurants, and the theater. Within a very short time, they became discontented with the limited living space and the lack of a yard and soon they were on the move again.

Whether you are looking at a bungalow, condo, or apartment, choose a design that has all the living space you need, including the laundry area, on one level. Even one step (e.g., a sunken living room) can become an obstacle if physical limitations develop; or it could be a potential hazard for unsuspecting visitors.

Should you buy a smaller home or a condominium or rent an apartment?

Here are some thoughts on each.

BUNGALOW

A widow and her mother purchased an adult lifestyle bungalow. Each had her own space and privacy. Many widows who live in the area are very supportive, which has enabled them to make many adjustments successfully.

Consider something that will likely appreciate in value and will be easy to sell if necessary. An attached garage with a stepless entry into the house is desirable. If there is a loft or basement suite, it could be useful for younger visitors. Often (but not always), you can have more privacy in a bungalow, and the noise level is more controlled. Renovations and landscaping are your decision. Pets are always welcome, and walking the dog begins at your door. You can usually choose your own cable or satellite provider. Parcels can be delivered right to your door. Taxes, heat, power, water, and garbage removal are the owner's responsibility. Additional costs include exterior maintenance, repairs, and yard work. Insurance companies require house checks if you are going away.

Building inspectors, realtors, and lawyers can fill important roles in safeguarding your purchase.

CONDOMINIUM

A condominium is space bounded by floors, ceiling, and walls that define your home. So your money will be invested in "real" property only. Choose a unit that can appreciate in value and be easy to sell if you move, or easy to settle your estate. Many people purchase condominiums because there is no yard work or exterior maintenance and they can lock the door and take off whenever they want. Northerners don't have to worry about shoveling snow!

Many condos are sold as a "lifestyle" rather than just an individual living unit. Some buildings have fitness rooms, party rooms, swimming pool, library, activity room, workshop, etc. Some have a fantastic location on water or in a city center. Gated communities are becoming popular and usually offer a higher level of security. Others offer varying degrees of security.

Along with taxes, you will also pay condominium fees, so find out how much they will be and what these fees cover. How are the condo fees assessed? Recently we heard of a situation where the fees were determined by the number of bedrooms and *not* by the size of the unit. As a result, people with a 1,000-square-foot unit were assessed the same amount as those with a 3,500-square-foot unit. They were unaware of this when they purchased their smaller unit. It was set in stone and they could do nothing about it.

Most condos hire a professional property management company. Find out who it is and check out their track record.

Can you live within the rules of the condo? In many condos, you need permission to do renovations to your own unit. Do you mind waiting for an elevator? Is the parking space suitable? If there is a balcony, are there restrictions on how you can use it? Barbeques are usually a no-no. Wise advice: When parking spaces are sold separately, invest in one, even if it's not needed. You may decide to rent it to someone for extra income. If you need to sell your condo, it will be easier to find a buyer if the condominium comes with a parking space.

Make sure there are no current or unsettled lawsuits against the condominium corporation.

Buying new

A new condo is often purchased from plans that you view at a "reception center." We have seen many condo buildings sell out before the developer even put a shovel in the ground! Make sure that everything agreed upon is in writing, e.g., guaranteed move-in date. Be cautious: completion date and move-in date can be different.

If possible, don't have two properties "close" on the same day. It is worth the investment to pay for bridge financing.[6] We have seen many seniors store their furniture and move into a hotel until their new home was finally finished. *Make sure you hire a lawyer who is an expert in the field of condominium law.*

---

6   When people own a second home for a short time until they receive the funds from the one they have sold, banks will give them a loan for the overlapping days. It is easier than trying to close one house and move into the other the same day, especially when you are older.

Further research can be done in bookstores or your local library. Check out the following Web site: *www.cci.ca.*[7]

APARTMENT

You will have no money invested in the apartment. If you have sold your home, you can invest your capital.

A lease is signed for a specific amount for a fixed period of time. There is usually a penalty to break the lease. Is there a "death clause" in your rental agreement that aids in ending the lease? How much notice must be given if you decide to move? Some owners allow their residents to sublet, while others do not.

You are not responsible for maintenance, repairs, or yard work. There are no taxes to pay. Again, you can lock the door and go away for as long as you like. There are various levels of security depending on the building you choose.

You usually will need permission to paint or even to change a light fixture. You may be limited in installing air conditioners, blinds, or drapes. If you have wall-to-wall carpeting installed, most buildings require that it be removed at your cost should you move. Often there are restrictions on balcony gardens. And again, barbeques are usually a no-no. Some permit pets, others don't. Some offer a guest suite you can rent when family or friends visit.

Helpful hint: When seniors purchase or rent properties with underground parking, they should make sure they can easily maneuver their car in and out of the tight corners and parking places. A test drive is mandatory. An eighty-four-year-old woman we know sold her large old car and bought a little red two-door. It was easy to drive and park. It also fulfilled her dream of owning her first "sports car"!

CHECKING OFF THE FEATURES YOU WANT

Which of these features in your bungalow, condo, or apartment do you want?

---

7   As well, here are two books that appear to be up to date on the subject: Kay Senay, *Condo Buying and Ownership Made Simple: Tips to Save Time and Money*; and Beth A. Grimm, *The Condo Owner's Answer Book*.

- One bedroom
- Two bedrooms
- Three bedrooms
- One bathroom
- A bathroom and a powder room
- Two bathrooms
- A bathtub
- A walk-in shower
- Grab bars in the bathroom
- Lots of storage space
- Drawers
- Patio
- Deck
- Balcony
- Air conditioning
- Gas heat
- Electric heat
- Gas fireplace
- Wood-burning fireplace
- Dining room
- Eat-in kitchen
- Open-concept kitchen
- Closed-off kitchen
- Stove supplied
- Refrigerator supplied
- Washer supplied
- Drier supplied
- Dishwasher supplied
- Room for a freezer
- Walk-in closet
- Linen closet
- Broom closet
- Storage in the unit
- Indoor parking
- Outdoor parking
- Parking for guests
- Wood floors
- Carpeting
- Ceramic floors
- Covered entrance
- Can drive up to the door
- Closed-circuit TV
- Doorman
- Security
- Elevator(s)
- No elevator
- Indoor swimming pool
- Outdoor swimming pool
- Workshop
- Library
- Activity room
- Guest suite available (Cost?)
- Pets permitted/not permitted
- Garbage chute
- Garbage room
- Manager living on-site
- Others (list)

LEARNING FROM OTHERS

Judy's dad was a builder and always said, "I know you plan to live there a long time but buy or build something you could sell if you had to." Our dream home was designed with a thirty-foot country kitchen, but no dining room. However, provisions were made so that part of the kitchen could become a formal dining room by opening up another doorway already "roughed" into the wall studs and installing a divider. The new owners did exactly that.

One lady sold her large home and chose an adult bungalow that would be mortgage-free. She wanted something that was convenient, rentable should she keep it as an investment, and easy to sell if necessary. Private space, in this case a loft, for children or grandchildren if they came to visit was also a priority. She really thought it through.

Doorways and hallways should be wide enough to accommodate walkers or wheelchairs, should they become necessary. Hallways should be at least forty-two inches wide, and doorways should be at least thirty-two inches. We had a call from a retired doctor and his wife who were planning to move to a three-bedroom apartment. As he used a wheelchair, we asked to borrow it to check out the apartment. It was next to impossible for the wheelchair to make the turn into either bathroom. We then looked at a two-bedroom apartment in the same building and the wheelchair maneuvered easily in and out of all the rooms. Although they wanted the extra bedroom, they wisely chose the smaller unit.

If the bathroom needs grab bars, can they be installed easily? More and more seniors are now looking at large walk-in showers or tubs with a seat rather than fancy tubs that are difficult to enter or exit. Another consideration for the bathroom is "pocket doors" that slide into the wall, or doors that open out. Many seniors fall in the bathroom, so it is important that someone can come to their aid quickly and not have difficulty getting help to them because they are blocking the door.

Seniors are encouraged to choose or install features that allow them to live independently and to be somewhat self-sufficient in their new home as long as possible.

Desirable features:

- Lever handles
- Lever faucets
- Electrical outlets that are located a little higher and easier to use
- Decora light switches
- Windows that open with levers rather than cranks
- Bathrooms and kitchens that are wheelchair- or walker-friendly

In the kitchen consider:

· Non-glare countertops with rounded edges
· Cabinets of convenient height
· Side-by-side refrigerator and freezer
· Appliance controls that can be used without reaching over hot surfaces
· A pantry
· Drawers that pull out easily for pots, etc.

Choose a home that has products and appliances requiring minimum maintenance.
Check for:

· Good lighting near doorways and stairwells
· Motion-sensitive exterior lights (a good security feature)

QUESTIONS TO ASK THE CURRENT CONDO- OR APARTMENT-DWELLERS

There is a variety of condominiums and apartments available. Talk to people in the buildings you are looking at and ask lots of questions such as, how do they enjoy living there, and do they have any complaints? Can you live with the rules and regulations for that particular building? Some of our seniors have had their names on lists waiting for specific units to become available. They liked the location and desired a certain floor plan. When their unit became available, they took it, sold their homes, and moved. They knew exactly what they wanted and were willing to wait until their ideal unit came along.

Make sure you know exactly what the financial commitments would be, and how easy or difficult it would be to sell or get out of the agreement should there be an unexpected illness or change in circumstances.

Look at the surrounding area. Are there any empty fields nearby? One man had a lovely balcony with a great view until they started building another condo only a few feet from his. A woman enjoyed her view until they built a shopping center near her. Now she sees the back of the mall and contends with the noise of delivery trucks in the middle of the night.

Some considerations

- If you choose a condo, how easy will it be to resell and get your money out of it?
- Is the building well maintained and in excellent condition?
- Are the exterior doors easy for seniors to open?
- Is it in a desirable location?
- Are there enough elevators?
- Is there an elevator large enough to handle your extra-large couch, mattress, etc.? (Our men had to carry a queen-size mattress and box spring up eleven flights of stairs because of an undersized elevator.)
- Will it be quiet or noisy?
- Is there parking? If so, do you pay for it?
- If no longer driving, can you rent out your parking space?
- Does the condo have a good reserve fund for major expenditures? (Such as roof repair.)
- Who pays for power and water?

A tip for adult children

Remember, parents do not like being told what to do. If you feel they are about to make an unwise decision, you need to think of questions that will make them stop and think. You could say, "Mom, I care what happens to you. Would you mind if I paid for a lawyer (building inspector, etc.) just to make sure everything is okay?" This way, you are showing concern, yet respecting her right to decide.

LUXURY LIVING ON WHEELS

The market for recreational vehicles has been growing. Some seniors with a sense of adventure are selling or storing belongings and heading down the road. They often spend winters in the south and head north for the summer. If you're competent at trouble-shooting and repairing vehicles, you can buy a motor home quite reasonably. You can also spend hundreds of thousands on a new luxury RV. **NOTE:** If you have any doubts about leaving your "treasures" and community, at least some possessions could be stored to help you start over.

RVs can have fully equipped kitchens, central vacuums, leather sofas, large flat-screen televisions, queen-size beds, skylights, retractable walls, heating, air conditioning, screened-in rooms, and more . . . Most people love the elevated seating that gives you a great view—especially over bridge railings and traffic ahead. Home-cooked meals are usually healthier, more diet-friendly, and more economical than what you can buy on the run. Ladies especially love having their own clean bathroom instead of having to use public "pit stops."

Some questions to think about:

- Is it easy to drive? Take it for a long test drive.
- Are the driving seats comfortable for you?
- Do you want an actual bedroom? Take off your shoes and try the bed. Is it comfortable?
- Do you plan to have visitors? Will they stay for a meal? Will they need a place to sleep?
- Is there a convenient place for a computer?
- Is there enough storage in the kitchen?
- Is there enough storage for clothing and linens?
- Are there privacy blinds or curtains?
- Is the bathroom easy to use?
- Is there a shower or tub?
- Is there enough storage in the bathroom? Is it accessible?
- Is the lighting sufficient?
- Is it easy to get in and out of the RV? Does the step retract easily?
- Is there exterior storage? (Look at the "basement model."[8]) Is it easily accessible? Is it lockable?
- Is it easy to fill the water tank?
- Is it easy to empty the holding tank?
- Can you tow a vehicle?
- Can you bring bikes if you want?
- Is there a warranty? What does it cover?
- How much will the insurance cost? What does it cover?

---

8 Basement model RVs have lots of exterior storage, usually fairly low down on the vehicle.

- How much will it cost for gas? Keep in mind you will be saving on restaurant food and lodgings.
- Would a diesel motor be a wiser choice? They are more costly to buy and repair but good for high mileage and more fuel efficient.
- Does it have air conditioning? Both engine and roof air (two on longer models) plus a built-in generator to power everything while in motion, or parked where there is no plug-in, is very desirable.

Whatever you are considering, list your priorities. Years ago, we were looking for a motor home with a queen-sized bed and a table that would seat five people comfortably. We had lots of calls from sales people. They would say, "It has central vac and a microwave."

We'd ask, "Does it have a queen-sized bed?"

"Well no. But it does have — "

If you make a list of what you're looking for, it's easier to see if it will meet your needs.

CHAPTER 5

Residences—What's Right for You or Your Parents?

MAJOR ADVANTAGES IN community living are: social interaction, proper food, housekeeping, supervised medical care, mental stimulation, physical safety, and physical activities. People decide to move for a variety of reasons, and this will be reflected in the type of residence they choose. With this in mind, start eliminating those places that can't or don't cater to your particular needs. We have had three calls this week from people who don't know what to do. They all have homes, have to move, and are in a state of panic. They don't know what options are out there and have no idea where to begin.

The sudden onset of serious health concerns can force a senior to take the first available retirement residence or long-term care facility. On the other hand, some have the luxury of choosing when and where to go. Continuing Care Retirement Communities cover the entire spectrum from independent apartments

to nursing care. They offer apartments, one- or two-bedroom suites, rooms with kitchenettes, studios, assisted living accommodations, and nursing-home care. Some complexes even have secure areas for people with various stages of Alzheimer's. Unfortunately, few facilities offer this complete range of care.

"Luxury independent living" is being marketed in many cities. It's like living in a five-star resort with pool, spa, gourmet meals, and available chauffeur. The person pays for only the services he or she uses because the "resorts" take only relatively healthy individuals looking for an easier adult lifestyle. This policy is supported by those who enjoy good health and who are more likely to choose a residence where everyone else is healthy. A place full of wheelchairs can be daunting for someone who is not at that stage. When major health concerns are the main issue, many facilities can be eliminated right away.

Some independent apartments provide few services, while others offer an amazing support system including meals, housekeeping, laundry services, nursing care, activities, spa, and valet parking. Independent, healthy, active people require no support, but the services are available, at extra cost, if health deteriorates. This avoids having to leave established friends and familiar surroundings when medical concerns develop. A good choice for those who do have health concerns is a facility that offers progressive stages of assisted living such as medical care, extra supervision, and possibly even help with eating and dressing.

Loneliness is a major incentive for aging people to move. It can be brought on by the loss of a mate, friends or family members moving away, or forced "hibernation" due to the summer heat or the snows of winter. People who are lonely should choose a place where there are planned activities, outings, and a central area where people are encouraged to come and socialize. When residents want privacy or quiet, they can retire to the confines of their own suite, yet socialize when so inclined. It's a win-win situation.

"Wanderers" with Alzheimer's or dementia need to live in a secure area where they are stimulated, treated with dignity and respect, and are able to go outside safely when the weather permits. Unfortunately, only a limited number of facilities offer this. Managers confide that they are simply not very profitable.

Are there nutrition and dietary concerns? Make sure the residence you have in mind is able to accommodate food sensitivities (e.g, low gluten or gluten-free, restricted salt, vegetarian, and so forth).

Many seniors "don't do mornings." Do they have to go to the dining room for breakfast or may they eat in their own suite? Can the staff bring them a tray of food? Is there an additional charge for this service? Can they supply their own breakfast?

After the type of facility has been determined, you can begin to narrow down the choices. The majority of residences have Web sites providing information easily and quickly. Most are willing to mail information to you when you request it. Ask them to include floor plans, price lists, medical care availability, and the variety of services and activities . Do your research.

We find the indecision of not knowing what to do can be exhausting, but the following should greatly assist your decision making. When you have narrowed down your choices to one or two places, it is important that you visit and eat a meal or two there. Most residences are quite happy to have you as their guest. It's also an opportunity to get a "feel" for the residence, people, and staff. If you or your loved one doesn't like the food, then of course, nothing else is going to matter. If a resort-inspired retirement residence is desired, bear that in mind as you make your assessment.

A TOUR OF THE BUILDING

As you go through, be sensitive to the following:

- Does the building seem clean and well maintained?
- Does the staff show a caring attitude toward the seniors?
- Do the staff members work well with each other as a team?
- Do they seem helpful?
- Do the residents and staff seem welcoming and friendly?
- How do some of the residents feel about their "home"? Talk to them.
- Are there many visitors or volunteers around? If possible, talk with them to find out how they feel about the building and staff.

Further considerations:

- Does the residence have a good reputation?
- Is a health assessment necessary?
- Can the staff handle mild dementia? (This concerns either your parent or their possible neighbor.)
- What security features do they have in place?
- What happens if health deteriorates?
- Can they give extra care for a fee?
- Can you pay for a private caregiver?
- Can they insist that you (or your parent) move if health does deteriorate?
- Are they willing to customize the suite to meet needs or desires? Is there a cost?
- Will they provide furniture? (for a fee)
- Is a cat permitted?
- Is a dog permitted?
- Is a bird permitted?
- Is the Internet available? (phone, cable, or wireless)
- Is there a computer available for resident use?
- Is there user-friendly technology that allows video conferencing with family members?
- Is cable provided?
- Are there daily activities?
- Is there an activity bus?

Important features or amenities:

- Is nursing care available?
- Is management on-site twenty-four hours per day?
- Is there front desk reception during the day?
- Is there front desk reception during the evening?
- Are there security cameras?
- Is there a full generator backup for power failures?
- Are wheelchairs permitted?
- Are walkers permitted?
- Are scooters permitted?
- May scooters be "parked" in the corridors?
- Is oxygen therapy permitted?
- Is there a warm, inviting entrance?

- Is the dining room attractive?
- Is there a private dining area for family functions?
- Are the lounges and sitting areas inviting and being used by the residents?
- Is smoking permitted? If so, where?
- May the resident use his/her own phone provider?
- May the resident use his/her own long-distance provider?
- Is it a location or building where a cell phone will work?

Extra amenities:

- Twenty-four-hour concierge?
- Valet parking?
- Library?
- Activity room?
- Fireplace?
- TV room?
- Large-screen theater?
- Beauty salon?
- Esthetician?
- Tuck shop?
- Chapel?
- Resident laundry facilities? Is there an additional cost?
- Wet bar?
- Pub?
- Piano lounge?
- Pool table?
- Fitness room?
- Swimming pool?
- Outdoor patio or garden?
- Private patio?
- Bright atrium?
- Craft room?
- Full kitchen that residents can book for baking?
- Workshop?
- Storage for seasonal clothing?
- Resident storage? (in their unit or in the building)
- Accessible parking?
- Wheelchair accessible entrances and exits?
- Air conditioning?
- Fire and smoke alarms and sprinklers?

May a toaster, coffeemaker or kettle be used in the room? We are finding that many residences are saying "NO TOASTERS." One morning we realized why. While moving a client in, we heard bells sounding in the hallways and sirens outside. We looked out the window just as two fire trucks arrived. When we could finally open the door to the hall, guess what? The smell of burnt toast was everywhere! The staff later told us they'd had three incidents of "burnt toast" that month.

Is the residence flexible enough to allow for an individual's lifelong habits? A friend likes her own pot of hot tea with a tea cozy. Each meal they bring her the small teapot and she puts her tea cozy on it. Some bring sugar-free jam for their toast. Others enjoy a glass of wine with their dinner. They provide the wine, and the staff graciously pours it for them.

SERVICES PROVIDED

- Number of meals daily
- Number of snacks daily
- Special diets accommodated
- In-room tray service
- Twenty-four-hour nursing
- Doctor on call
- Foot care available
- Lab services available
- Pharmacy services available
- Physiotherapy available
- Supervision of medication
- Housekeeping (weekly)
- Housekeeping (daily)
- Laundry services (linens)
- Laundry services (personal)
- Dry cleaning services available
- Alterations available
- On-site banking
- Recreation programs
- Activity director
- Accessible minibus available for outings
- Transportation for medical appointments (Is there a charge?)
- Weekly church services
- Other

COSTS

- What is the basic monthly rate?
- What was the rate increase over the past two years?
- Do you pay for only the services used? (Can you save by making up your own bed and by providing your own breakfast?)
- What are the additional charges?

Cable TV	*Guest meals*
Utilities	*Medication supervision*
Phone	*Resident transportation*
In-room tray service	*Movie nights*
Help with baths	*Beauty salon*
Help with dressing	*Escort to meals*
Assistance with ambulation	*Minor services (e.g., putting*
Setting off the fire alarm	*up a picture)*
(burned toast . . .)	

Important questions to ask:

- Are there any tax credits?
- Do you sign a contract?
- May you keep a copy of it?
- How much notice needs to be given if you (or your parent) want or need to move?
- How quickly must the suite be emptied in the event of a death?
- What are the charges after death?
- Do you (or your parent) get a discount if away on vacation?
- Can you sublet your furnished suite for the winter?
- Do you (or your parent) get a discount if in the hospital?
- Are you allowed to let someone use the room (and services) if you are away?
- Can a family member stay in the suite for a few nights? (Cost?)
- Is there a furnished suite for a visiting family member? (Cost?)
- Could you return for a complimentary meal?
- Is a two- or three-day trial stay possible? (Cost?)
- Could you have a sample menu, a newsletter, or an activity calendar?

If you are fortunate enough to have the choice of a particular room or suite:

- Is the morning or afternoon sun preferred?
- Would the preferred view be a busy street or a quiet garden?
- Is it important to bring a specific piece of furniture? (e.g., piano, china cabinet, large bed)
- Is it important that a family member sleep over occasionally?
- Is high-speed Internet a priority?
- Is it better to be closer (less distance) or farther from the elevator (noise)?
- Is indoor parking needed?
- Are activities for visiting grandchildren a consideration?

CHECKING OUT A SUITE

Look for:

- Keyless entry
- Suitable size
- Suitable layout
- Desirable view
- Windows that open
- Emergency response system

- Individual temperature controls (for heat and air conditioning)
- Sufficient cupboard space
- Sufficient shelves in cupboard
- Permission to decorate (paint, put up a border)
- Window coverings supplied
- A fireplace
- Wood floors
- Clean carpets
- Balcony
- Patio
- In-room safe
- A small fridge supplied
- A microwave supplied
- Flat-screen TV

We find it handy to take a checklist with us when we are planning a move into a retirement residence. Here is our list to take with you to help you remember some of the important details.

Living area

- Is there room for a sofa, love seat, chairs?
- Electrical outlets — where? How many?
- Where does the television go?
- Who orders cable?
- Where does the phone go?
- Are there overhead lights?
- Is there wall space for pictures?
- Is there space for a china cabinet?
- Is there space for a buffet?
- Is there a place to park a walker?
- Other questions?

Bedroom area

- What size bed will fit?
- What is the best place for a bed?
- Do you need to supply sheets? Blankets?
- How many dressers will fit?
- Is there room for a chair?
- Where would the television go?
- Are there overhead lights?
- Where does the phone go?
- Is there room for a desk?
- Is there room for a computer?
- Who is the Internet provider?

- How much cupboard space is there?
- Are there shelves in the cupboard?
- Is there wall space for pictures?
- Are the window coverings adequate?
- Electrical outlets — where? How many?
- Other questions?

Kitchenette

- Are the cupboards accessible for a senior?
- Is there a sink?
- Is there counter space?
- Are there drawers?
- Is a fridge supplied? If not, is there space for one?
- Is a microwave supplied? If not, is there space for one?
- Are there accessible electrical outlets? Where are they?
- Is the lighting sufficient?
- Is there room for a small table and chair(s)?
- Other questions?

Bathroom

- Can a walker or wheelchair get into the bathroom?
- Is there a call button?
- Are there grab bars?
- Is there a tub or a shower?
- Is a rubber mat needed for the tub or shower?
- Do you need to supply a bath seat?
- Is a shower curtain needed?
- Are there enough towel bars?
- Do you supply the towels?
- Do you supply the toilet paper?
- How much cupboard space is there?
- Are there drawers?
- Is there room for a laundry hamper?
- Other questions?

Balcony

- Is it easily accessible? (Is there a step?)
- Is it covered?
- Will it take two chairs?

- Will it take a table?
- Is there room for plants?
- Is the door to the balcony secure?
- Other questions?

Window coverings

- Are they supplied?
- Can blinds be installed?
- Can a valance be put up?
- Other questions?

Decorating

- Can the color of paint be chosen?
- Can wallpaper be hung?
- Can a border be hung?
- Is there a choice in floor covering?
- Can blinds be installed?
- Can a valance be installed?
- Other questions?

Pets

- Are pets permitted?
- Are seeing-eye dogs permitted?
- Is there room for a pet and pet supplies?
- Can you pay someone to help with pet care if needed?
- Other questions?

Suggested items to have in a kitchenette
(to allow some in-room snacks and entertaining)

- Coffee
- Coffee maker
- Tea
- Kettle
- Sugar
- Sugar substitute
- Sugar bowl
- Mugs
- Juice
- Canned drinks
- Glasses
- Wineglasses
- Plates (often four)
- Dessert plates
- Cake plate
- Bowls
- Jam
- Cookies
- Cookie tin
- Crackers

- Forks
- Spoons
- Knives (plus a sharp knife)
- Cutting board
- Vitamins
- Cereal
- Milk
- Placemats
- Can opener
- Toaster
- Microwave
- Small tray
- Detergent
- Dishtowels
- Plastic wrap
- Baggies
- Flower vase
- Other

Important considerations

- A kettle that turns off automatically
- No candles (one forgetful person can affect a hundred lives)
- No bleach (one drop on the carpet can necessitate replacing the whole thing)
- No frayed cords on old lamps (replace the cord if you insist on keeping the lamp)
- Bookshelves attached to the wall
- No area rugs on carpets (in most cases)
- Furniture arranged so no sharp corners are sticking out
- No sharp objects placed carelessly in drawers
- Handrails for the bathroom (if needed)
- No glass in bathroom (you can get nice plastic cups)
- A night light for the bathroom

FROM OUR FILES

A lady called to ask us to move her. We had moved the couple several years before from a very large, expensive home to a large, high-priced suite in a retirement residence. She really didn't want to move but knew she had to because she had become a widow, had spent most of the money they had received from the sale of their home, and needed to cut back on monthly expenses.

People are living longer and we see lots of seniors who have "outlived" their money. They had moved to the largest suite in the most expensive residence, then realized those "extra years" were draining their finances. Many tell us they never expected to live so long! It's better to choose a more modest place that you can stay in indefinitely. Some people rent the smallest room possible in the best residence they can find. They don't plan to spend much time in it anyway!

Recently, we visited a charming ninety-year-old lady who lived in a very tiny yet very full room. Her day bed was custom built so there was lots of storage under it. She had a corner cabinet, an armoire, a computer, three small chairs, and lots of pictures, plants, and "precious things." Her room was reasonable, welcoming, and home!

FOR ADULT CHILDREN

You want your parents to feel involved in the decision-making process, but don't give them a choice that is not available. Don't give them an option for total independent living when their doctor has said they need medication supervision. Don't suggest they can bring a pet if they can't. Involve them in as many realistic decisions as you can. It helps them to feel at least somewhat in control and they make the transition easier and settle in faster.

Try to have a sense of humor in the midst of it all. At times we will say, "Of course you can bring that. We'll just knock out a hole in the wall and use some of the next suite!" Usually they laugh and realize it's not possible.

For extra nursing care and more supervised help with daily living, many people will choose a nursing home or a long-term care facility.

CHAPTER 6

Choosing a Nursing Home

SEVERAL YEARS AGO, we received a call from the hospital informing us that Doug's mom was being discharged and we were to pick her up by ten a.m. Judy said, "No!" She knew that Mother couldn't go home, and picking her up meant bringing her to our home and placing her way down on "the waiting list" for a nursing home. We had tried looking after her and found ourselves to be totally ill equipped.

Judy told them, "If you have a placement for her, we will pick her up and take her there, but if there isn't one available, then we will wait until there is." They quickly had a spot for her!

A nursing home is a place where health care services and help with daily living are provided. More care is provided than the senior can easily and reasonably get at home or in most retirement residences.

Each nursing home is different. Some are beautiful and new, while others are very old and at times quite smelly! Some are warm, inviting, and friendly, while others seem cold and intimidating. Most have private rooms but others have two, three, and even four people sharing one room. There are rooms with a private bathroom, while in many places there is a shared bathroom. Some have government financial aid and some don't. Some require a deposit to keep a room available.

THINGS TO THINK ABOUT AS YOU BEGIN YOUR SEARCH FOR A NURSING HOME

Location

- Familiar area
- A safe community
- Convenient for visitors
- Near public transportation
- Parking for visitors
- Near shopping if mobile
- Other

First impressions

- Welcoming
- Clean
- Well lit
- Well maintained
- Attractive
- Homey
- Fresh smelling but not from heavy chemicals concealing the smell of urine. (You might smell urine near some rooms but it should not be the dominant smell in the building.)

The grounds

- Are they well maintained?
- Is there a place to walk?
- Is there a place to sit?
- Are they secure?
- Are they safe?
- Are they accessible in daytime only?
- Are they accessible in good weather only?
- Is smoking permitted in this area?

Residents (positive and negative impressions)
Ask residents if they have any complaints.

- Content
- Clean
- Well groomed
- Restrained
- Involved
- Peaceful
- Alone in rooms
- Pleased with the place
- Wearing appropriate clothing for the season
- Interacting with other seniors
- Interacting with staff
- Sitting slumped in a chair sleeping (lack of stimulation)
- Shouting (can be very unsettling)
- Moaning
- Other impressions

Staff

- Friendly
- Cheerful
- Treat residents with respect
- Seem to "care" about residents
- Neat and well groomed
- Ratio in the daytime
- Ratio at night
- Other

Safety

- Entrance wheelchair- or walker-friendly (a door that opens easily and stays open long enough for the senior to navigate through it)
- Smoke alarms
- Fire doors
- Well-marked exits
- Hallways clear and uncluttered
- Grab bars in hallways and bathrooms
- Good lighting
- Elevators that are wheelchair- or walker-friendly
- Elevators with large, easily read operating buttons
- Emergency call buttons or cords near beds and in all bathrooms
- An emergency evacuation plan in place
- Locked exit doors that would be automatically released by a fire alarm. Also a code that any staff member could use to open a locked door.
- Other

Health care

- Is there a nurse on duty twenty-four hours per day?
- Can the senior keep his/her own doctor?
- Is there a doctor on call?
- Does the resident physician make regular visits?
- Is there a charge to give out medications? (How much?)
- Is foot care available? (Cost?)
- Is physiotherapy available? (Cost?)
- Is speech therapy available? (Cost?)

- Is hydrotherapy available? (Cost?)
- Is there a restorative care program?
- Other considerations?

The room — features

- Private room
- Shared room
- Private bathroom with shower
- Private bathroom without shower
- Shared bathroom
- Storage place in bathroom
- Wheelchair-friendly
- Adequate lighting
- Connection for phone
- Connection for cable
- Room temperature controllable
- Air conditioning for summer
- A lockable drawer

The room — questions and considerations

- What personal furniture may the resident bring?
- What storage is available?
- May the resident use his/her own sheets? (Who will wash them?)
- How is privacy guarded from "wanderers"?
- How are valuables guarded from wanderers?
- Does the resident have to label clothing?
- Does the facility prefer to label the clothing?
- Can the resident put up pictures?
- Does the nursing home prefer to put them up? (Cost?)
- Does the maintenance person check all electrical cords before you can plug them in?

Food

Food and mealtimes are often the highlight of the day, so this section merits careful attention.

- Is there a dietitian on staff?
- Is the kitchen inspected regularly by the health department?

- Is there choice and variety in the meals?
- Is the home able to accommodate special diets? (e.g., vegetarian, lactose-intolerant, heart-healthy, diabetes, Kosher, no eggs, no wheat . . .)
- Are there three meals a day? (Ask to see a typical menu.)
- Are there three snacks a day? (What typical snacks are served? When and where?)
- Are the dining areas pleasant?
- Are the tables inviting?
- Do the meals look appetizing?
- Are seats at the tables assigned? If so, do they try to put compatible people together?
- Is there a private dining area?
- Can a visitor stay for a meal? (Cost? How much notice needs to be given?)
- Can the resident have food in the room?
- Can the resident have a fridge in the room?
- Can the resident make a hot drink in the room?
- Can food be brought in? (His/her favorite Chinese food? A birthday cake?)
- Is help provided to get to the dining room if needed? (Cost?)
- Is help provided with feeding if needed? (Cost?)
- Is alcohol permitted in the room?
- Other considerations?

Visitors

When Judy's grandmother had a stroke and landed in a nursing home, she didn't want to see anyone. The truth was, she didn't want anyone to see her. Counseling was needed.

- Is there a social worker on staff?
- What are the visiting hours?
- Are visitors or family members invited to be involved in any of the activities?
- Is there a family council?
- If so, how often does it meet?
- Are families able to voice their concerns? How?
- Can residents be taken for outings?

Activities

- Is there an activity director?
- Is there an activity room?
- What are the weekly activities?
- What are the special activities?
- Are the daily or weekly activities posted?
- What exercise activities are encouraged?
- Is there a craft room?
- Do volunteers help with the activities?
- Are the seniors encouraged to be involved in activities?
- Is there an activity bus for outings? Is it wheelchair-friendly?
- Are there activities that meet physical, mental, emotional, and spiritual needs?
- Is group singing encouraged?
- Is there a library?
- Is there a chapel?
- Is there an area for movies?
- Are pets permitted to visit?
- Is there a computer available for the seniors to use?
- Can someone help the resident send an e-mail to a loved one?
- Other considerations?

WHAT INFORMATION IS REQUIRED?

- A medical form filled out by a doctor
- Financial statements showing the ability to meet the commitments or entitlement to government assistance
- Personal information on power of attorney for care and finances, next of kin, etc.

THE CONTRACT

Ask to see a copy of the contract. Is a deposit needed to hold the room? How much is it and what does it cover?

- What are the costs?
- What is covered?
- What is not covered?
- When are payments due?
- Is it a month-to-month agreement?

- How often can the rates go up?
- What is the responsibility of the resident?
- What are the rights of the residents?
- Are subsidies available?
- Will the home help relocate a senior to another room, floor, or residence? (Cost?)
- If a senior is in hospital for an extended time, can his/her room be given to someone else?
- Is a monthly statement provided?
- If the senior dies, what is the financial commitment to the nursing home?
- If the senior dies, how soon after does the room need to be emptied?
- Other questions?

NOTE: Your final choice will be a facility that comes closest to meeting all expectations with as few "downsides" as possible. Frequently there is little time to decide whether to accept it when a room becomes available.

THE ROOM — MAKING "FOUR WALLS" MORE LIKE HOME!

The reality is, there are many elderly people in hospitals waiting to be discharged into long-term care. They won't be going home! Another reality is that when a space is available, it will often be little more than four walls, a hospital bed, and maybe an institutional chair and/or dresser.

How sad! Even sadder is the fact that many elders seem ready to accept this. In fact, when help is first offered, some are quite insistent that you do nothing. We see this attitude reflected in such scenarios as bringing them their TV and being told, "No! Take it away. I don't want it."

A day or two later, guess what? Back we go with the TV.

Incidents such as this add to the roller coaster of emotions that families often go through. The good news is that following this, the senior becomes a little more open to allowing you to add a few "touches" to her room. Your goal of course is to make her room more like home.

Before proceeding, it should be noted that if you are fortunate enough to have some lead time, the following suggestions can be implemented before the senior arrives. Then his first impression has more of a chance of being positive rather than negative.

In our experience, the first things the resident should see are familiar, comfort-giving things on the wall and elsewhere, such as pictures of family, friends, pets, holidays, awards, medals, special certificates, etc. Along with the comfort factor, it gives the care staff topics for some friendly chit-chat.

As for the room in general, stand back and have a good look.

- Can the bed be moved to open up more usable space?
- How much wall space is there?
- Where will the TV go? Is there room for a familiar curio cabinet or bookcase, small table, his reading machine, his own dresser, a favorite chair, an extra chair for a visitor, a small fridge, a filing cabinet . . . ?
- Can he bring his computer? Is the Internet available in his room?

Some things to consider bringing: a favorite comforter or bedspread, their own pillows, an afghan, cookie tin, coffee mug, flower vase, books or magazines, playing cards, photo albums, bulletin board, calendar, magnifying glass, stuffed animal . . .

If your loved one has dementia and wants to bring some things that are valuable then put them in a locked cabinet. When you visit, you can reassure her that the items are still there, that they haven't been stolen or gotten lost. Some places allow you to bring a glass curio cabinet, while other places permit absolutely no glass. Check before you move mirrors or pictures with glass.

Whatever you decide to do, the end result should be a warmer, homier, and more familiar environment to help your loved one settle in.

CHAPTER 7

Approaches for Adult Children if Their Parents Have to Leave Their Home

RECENTLY WE WERE WITH a geriatric social worker who had spent her career working with seniors. She mentioned that the first thing a baby has is emotional memory. The last thing to go is also emotional memory. Some adults may have been abused as babies and have never overcome the associated bad emotional memories. With this in mind, it is important to speak quietly when discussing a move with your loved one, be it your husband, your wife, or your parent. Don't say, "You *have* to move!" Instead, think of the emotional side. "You will be looked after" . . . "You will be safe" . . . "They will make sure you get the proper amount of insulin" . . . "They will make your meals" . . . "If you have a chest pain in the middle of the night, you can push a button and someone will come to help right away." And so on.

Remember, your parent is your parent, not your "child." Parents need to be treated with dignity and respect. Don't bully, manipulate, or talk down to them. Involve them in the decision-making process, yet narrow the process down to manageable decisions. Expect some resistance. If you strongly believe that they should move, there are ways to soften them to the possibility. If your elders want to avoid the topic, and it's not an emergency, try again at a later time. If there is a health or safety issue, firmly, but with compassion, say, "We need to deal with this now." Try and give your loved ones a sense of involvement and control over their lives. Involving people your parents respect, such as a pastor, doctor, attorney, or close family friend might be helpful.

SUGGESTED STRATEGIES IF A MOVE IS NECESSARY

"I know that you don't want to move to a retirement residence but your doctor feels that you need a support system twenty-four hours a day. Why don't we check out what is available and see what they offer and what it costs? Maybe they would let you stay a couple of days before making any decision. You can enjoy the privacy of your own room, yet have the care you need when you need it."

"Mother, several times lately you have mentioned that you really don't want to cook anymore. You've also said that you are tired of being alone. I've been watching them build the new seniors' residence and I've done some reading about it. They say that all the meals are made on-site and are really great. Why don't we go and have lunch there and see if it might be right for you?"

"Dad, you've been looking after Mom for three years. We're really concerned about something happening to you, and if so what would happen to Mom? She could end up in an institution somewhere. Perhaps you should consider moving where there is help available, yet you can still be together. It would be easier on both of you."

"Mom, we're concerned about Dad. He's been very busy looking after you since the stroke you had three years ago. He's been shopping, cooking, cleaning, doing the laundry, and feeding you. He loves you so very much. He wants to be with you and look after you, but if something happened to him, you'd end up in an institution somewhere. I know he has some help, but it sure seems to be taking a toll on him. I think you should look at moving to the residence over by the grocery store. You would still be in a familiar area and you would have the help that is needed."

"Dad, I know you don't want to move yet, but I believe *you know* that it is time to move."

"Mom, I hear that your best friend, Mary, has moved to the Lodge. Have you talked with her? You should see how she is doing. Why don't you have lunch with her and see how she is?"

"Mom, I'm retiring in three months, and we're planning to go away for the winter. I think we should look at a place where you will have company and some meals if you want. I will be able to enjoy my retirement much more if I know that you are okay. We plan to get a place where you could come and visit for a couple of weeks in January or February. You could just lock the door and come. The new residence also has video conferencing, and we could see each other as we talk several times a week."

"We're going away for a week this winter. We would enjoy our holiday more knowing that you are okay. We've checked with the new residence and they have a room for the week. You only need to bring some clothes. We'll be back on the Friday and we'll all go out for dinner before we take you home." (When the week is over, don't ask too many questions. Thank them for helping you to have a relaxing holiday.)

The waiting lists for residences are getting longer. One residence in our area has forty-eight names on their waiting list. Each person has put a thousand dollar deposit just to be on the list. Tell your mom that right now she is fine in her home but someday she might not be.

"Let's see what is out there so you can at least get your name on a list. If one does come available, you don't have to take it."

An only child had an elderly parent with some "forgetfulness." It was necessary to move, but she was determined to stay in the house that she had lived in for fifty years. We told her that her son loved her very much and that he worried a lot about her. If she moved where there was help twenty-four hours a day, it would give him peace of mind, and he wouldn't have to worry about his mom lying alone on the floor for hours if she had a fall. Although she didn't want to, she moved "for her son." She actually became more peaceful once the decision to move was a reality.

> "Mom, the doctor says that you have to go somewhere to recover from your broken hip. Would you prefer the place on Main Street or the place by the new elementary school?

Never lie to your loved one even if he or she has Alzheimer's.

Don't say he is going to stay for only a few days when in reality he will not be going home. Although Alzheimer's patients have short-term memory loss, they seem to remember your words that it was to be "only for a few days." Frequently they will ask when someone is coming to take them home and state that they "promised."

TIP: If your parents are agitated and angry when you arrive and you want to discuss a move, start with a diversion. An example is, "You can't believe what happened! I went to the store to get your favorite cookies and was getting ready to pull into a parking spot. A little red car came speeding out of nowhere and zoomed into my spot. I was right there ready to pull in and my spot was gone! Can you believe it?" You are taking their mind off themselves and letting them share your anger. We have had success with diversions.

CHAPTER 8

Intergenerational households

SHOULD A PARENT MOVE IN WITH A CHILD?

Two women we worked with lived in their respective homes for eighty-four years. Yes, eighty-four years! Both women had moved into their grandparents' homes as babies along with their parents. Each ended up inheriting the family home. Years ago, it was normal for two or three generations to live in the same residence, for a variety of reasons. Often widows were only fifty or sixty years old when they moved in with a child and his/her family, but now a parent can be eighty or ninety.

Today, few parents want to give up their independence, let alone give it up to live with a child.

We designed our home with a potential granny suite for Doug's parents. It was never discussed, we just did it! As it turned out, they did *not* want to live with us. However, when Doug's mom ended up in the hospital, his aging dad did stay with us for a while. He preferred one of the children's bedrooms, so our oldest son got to be "granny."

Grandpa couldn't be left on his own, as he had some memory loss, but was content as long as we were close by and he had our undivided attention. Judy wasn't working at the time, so she got to entertain him with many games of cards, drives in the country, and endless repetitive conversations.

The mother-in-law of the President of the United States lives with her family in the White House.

Is this a growing trend? Yes — because of the current economy. Some adult children have been subsidizing retirement resident living for their senior parents; but they have now lost their jobs or seen their portfolios decimated. They are no longer able to help their parents and some can even use the financial help that a parent could provide by moving in and paying "rent." Some adult children also need parents to move in and help with the child care, if they are able.

In the twenty-first century, because of lack of finances, family expectations, emotional attachments, or cultural assumptions, parents still move in with a child. If there is no other choice or if it is something that you really want to do, can you make it work?

If you are single, it is sometimes easier to accommodate a parent. If your partner is not onside, it will be very challenging. Somehow the partner needs to see some benefits or "silver lining" from the arrangement; for example, some of the "rent" money could be used for a holiday, car, new TV, or boat.

An elderly client went to live with her daughter. Everyone was excited about it, yet a week later, a frantic call came: "The house is too small for all of us! We never realized how small it really is!" The reality was, they couldn't get along together in limited quarters for an extended period of time.

Although not always the case, in most situations you can see a parent deteriorating and have some time to plan ahead. We suggest you ask him to come visit for a week. Don't even mention living with you permanently. Following this "trial period," any thought about moving in might quickly fade. If not, carefully consider the long-term commitment you could be making. Will you be able to care for him if his health deteriorates or dementia gets a lot worse? What has your relationship been in the past and what is it now? Will other family members resent your relationship? Will they think you have ulterior motives? Will they offer backup support that will allow you some time out or a holiday?

Sit down with members of the household. Find out what concerns and aggravations each person has. Actually take a piece of paper and divide it in half. On one half, write the positive things about the potential arrangement and on the other half write the negative things. Can you live with or overcome the negative things? Be sure it's a family decision (positive or negative) none of you will regret later.

IS YOUR HOME ADAPTABLE?

Do you have a home in which your parent could have her own room with her own bathroom? If not, could you have some renovations done within your budget? Many parents are very thrifty, and you might have to pay for the renovations yourself. You can also see if government financial help is available. Some families have given a parent the master bedroom with bathroom ensuite so they could have a spacious bed-sitting room. Make sure their living space isn't near the bedroom you will use, as it is important that all members of the household have private space.

BRINGING YOUR PARENTS ONSIDE

If you believe they could move in with you, introduce the idea slowly and gently during general conversations. Talk to your parents with patience and respect. Even if you have never communicated well with them before, you need to now. Although you are the child and the caregiver and they are the parents, you need an adult-to-adult relationship. Don't be offended if they say "no." The timing just might not be right or something else might work better for everybody.

FINANCES

Do you have the finances to support them? Will other family members offer financial support? If they don't, will you resent it?

Finances need to be discussed and there must be a financial arrangement. Contributing at least a token amount can be a pride-saver for the seniors. Treat the arrangement as a business. They should pay a specific amount that is *fair to both parties* on the first day of each month. (We have seen some children bitter that the "subsidized" parent gave extravagant gifts to siblings or grandchildren who "didn't deserve it.") Agree on what you will pay for and what they will pay for (cable, their own phone line, food, transportation, medications, etc.).

MAKING IT WORK

Your parents need to know that you need to be fair to yourself as well as all members of the household. They are joining the team, not taking over! Make sure they understand that your job or family is important and has to come first. You are willing to make some adjustments but not willing to sacrifice either for them. It is a privilege and not a right for them to live with you.

AVOIDING MISUNDERSTANDINGS

- In their own living quarters, can they live as they want? (If it is messy, but not dangerous, is that their business? If they drink but are not abusive, is that their business?)
- Can they smoke? (Are there any restrictions?)
- Can they have visitors at any time? Where can they visit? Can visitors sleep over? (Where?)
- Can they bring a pet? Who cleans up?
- Can they bring their own car? Where do they park it?
- Will loss of hearing bother anyone? (Higher television volume if they won't use earphones.)

"TOGETHER TIME"

- Do they eat all meals with you or only some of them?
- Will you spend every evening together?
- Do they go to their room after dinner (so you can have time alone)?
- If you have friends over for dinner, do your parents join you?
- Do they go on holidays with you? If not, who "parent-sits"?

INDEPENDENCE

- Can they still make some of their own meals?
- If family members are still working, will they have difficulty with loneliness, especially if they are in a strange city?
- Can they still drive?
- Can they drive your car?
- How do they get to appointments (you, taxi, public transportation)?
- Can they take their own medications?
- Do they need help with bathing?

HOW CAN THEY BECOME A USEFUL PART OF THE HOUSEHOLD?

Are there meaningful things you could do as a family while they are living with you? Some families have written down stories about growing up years ago, while others have worked on their genealogy. A wise man had his mother look after all his plants, and she did a fabulous job.

Even in a wheelchair, a woman could help fold laundry or put the dishes in the dishwasher. She could help with the cooking or at least put supper in the oven. There are many ways an extra hand could be rewarding for everyone concerned.

HOW LONG CAN THEY STAY WITH YOU?

Some families have hired a "sitter" or a nurse so their parents wouldn't have to move. What is the cost? Know your limitations and communicate them. Let them know that although you wish it were different, if they become bedridden and need twenty-four-hour nursing assistance, you would have to find a caring place that could look after them properly.

As we write this, we are in the process of moving a mom out of a suite in a child's home. Words were spoken in frustration and anger and they might never reconcile. The daughter had excellent intentions, but a more realistic assessment should have been made beforehand.

If a parent or child is OPINIONATED, NEGATIVE, OR MANIPULATIVE, it will take a lot of effort to make it work . . . if at all!

SETTLING IN

If your parents have a kitchenette in their living space, you can provide meals for them to warm up. Perhaps they could have a meal a day with you. How will you handle weekends? (One lady made desserts on weekends and enjoyed them with her parents in their suite.)

- Have a cupboard with some snacks and a small fridge for them.
- When they are settling in, don't jump through hoops for them—the pattern you set is the pattern they will expect.
- Don't visit twenty-four hours a day—it is harder to cut back once you start.
- Look at the day-away programs that many areas provide. It gives them a break and something new to talk about.
- If they become verbally or emotionally abusive, limit your time or your children's time with them. You can tell your children that

grandma or grandpa has mental limitations and isn't aware of what she/he is doing. Draw the line if the abuse is physical or sexual. Don't sacrifice your children for your parents.

ADAPTING YOUR HOME FOR A PARENT WITH ALZHEIMER'S

- Put locks on exterior doors. Place them above or below eye level.
- Remove lock from bathroom door.
- Have at least one chair with arms for him to use.
- Remove rocking chairs.
- Keep pills locked away.
- Keep counters somewhat empty (put away things she could drink or hurt herself or someone else with, e.g., knives).
- Remove precious or breakable items.
- Remove furniture from the center of the room.
- Cover or remove mirrors (the person he sees may seem to be a stranger, and that can be frightening).
- Have quiet music rather than loud, disturbing programs on the television.
- Have something "familiar" on her bedroom door.

ADULT DAY-CARE

Several years ago, people tried setting up adult day-care centers. It was a great idea but before its time. Recently, some large businesses realized that employees were missing a lot of time trying to care for aging parents. They implemented adult day-care facilities for their employees' parents, and the feedback is encouraging. They have snacks and lunch and lots of activities. Some seniors' centers and retirement residences have day-away programs for people with Alzheimer's and even supply transportation if needed. Some of the activities include crafts, computer training, Scrabble, walks in the neighborhood, movie time, exercises, current event discussions, pottery, and cards.

If a child or a spouse is the only caregiver for someone with Alzheimer's disease, the day-away program gives them a much-needed break.

FROM OUR FILES

A widower was so happy! His daughter was coming to live with him! He was very lonely and looking forward to sharing his home.

Judy was curious. "Will she be paying rent?"

"No," he replied.

"Why not?" Judy asked.

"I can afford to let her stay with me," he answered.

"Do you have other children? What if you give her free room and board and she buys a new car or goes on an expensive trip? Would it upset your other children?"

Silence . . .

"If you have a girlfriend, would you like your daughter to join the two of you for *all* meals? If she has a boyfriend, may he sleep in your home? Where? If you had a stroke and needed money to go to a nursing home, what would happen to the house and your daughter?

"I'd never thought of those things," he said. "I'm glad we talked."

Another widower, Sam,[9] was ninety years old and wanted to remain in his own home. His daughter and her husband moved in. A while later, the unexpected happened — Sam's granddaughter and her husband broke up. After the marriage breakup, the judge gave Sam's live-in daughter and her husband custody of their baby grandchild. Now this elderly gentleman doesn't have much time with his very busy daughter, and the house is never peaceful or quiet. He's unhappy, frustrated, and doesn't know what to do.

Recently we have heard of several cases where a child or family had moved into the parent's home. This is not always discussed with siblings, it is "just done." We have seen parents sign over their home to a child, on the condition that the child would always look after them in their own home. What if the child dies, and his or her partner inherits the house and tells the seniors to leave?

---

9 His name has been changed.

Unfortunately, health conditions can deteriorate to the point that the family cannot care for the parent effectively. If a parent has to move to a care facility, where does the money come from if they have little available cash? We suggest that all parties carefully consider this option before any commitment is made.

BEWARE!

Our advice to adult children: communicate with your parents effectively and frequently so that someone does not take advantage of them. Keep them up to date on fraud schemes. Say something like, "Mom, you're not going to believe what I heard on the radio today . . ." If you tell them to be careful, they can be offended that you would think they could be so stupid as to fall for something.

An older relative, always wise and well informed, later in life fell victim to an "I should have known" mail fraud. Loss of pride and so much money hastened his death.

CHAPTER 9

Selling Your Home

MOST PEOPLE WANT to get the best possible price when they sell their home, although we've had a few seniors who preferred to have a "nice family" move into their neighborhood and purposely chose a lower offer. Some have also sold or given their home to a family member.

Each of our children would have bought our family home when we sold it, but couldn't afford it at the time. Recently we worked with an only child who was quite disappointed that his mother had listed the family home, but before she could tell him, it was sold in ten hours. He had grown up in the house and had been considering retiring and buying it if and when it ever came up for sale. Unfortunately, he lived out of town and had never discussed his intentions with his mom. He mentioned his disappointment to us but didn't feel he could tell her.

When selling your home, there are some things you can't change. The location (good or bad), style, and size of the house are fixed. There are, however, many things you can repair or improve to ensure you get the best price possible. Most realtors will give you some helpful suggestions and may bring in a "stager" who, for a fee, will make the right changes to ensure your home shows well. They can de-clutter, organize minor repairs or major renovations, and even supply appropriate furnishings and artwork to upgrade an interior so the house will sell quickly and for top dollar.

Many seniors refuse to have their lives inconvenienced by changes before they move, and others will not consider paying for the service.

DRIVE-BY APPEAL

This is very important! If people don't like the exterior of a home, they might not even consider making an appointment to view it.

How does your home measure up?

· Does it look tidy and well cared for?
· Does the front door and/or garage door need a fresh coat of paint?
· Is the grass cut?
· Do the shrubs and hedges need trimming?
· Are the flower beds well cared for?
· Does the driveway need sealing or sweeping?
· Does the walk need sweeping?
· Are there missing shingles?
· Are there black mildew marks on the house that need to be removed?
· Is the house number visible?
· Is any paint peeling?
· Is the mailbox worn? (Remove it or replace it.)
· Do any windows need repairs or upgrading?
· Is there a broken gutter?
· Are all spider webs removed?
· Are the exterior lights working? Are they dated?
· Other considerations?

REMEMBER: The first impression is important. (One lady we worked with loved the little improvements so much she confessed to having some second thoughts about selling.)

DE-CLUTTER

Something you can do that costs nothing but your time is to remove clutter and personal items such as family pictures. Since you're moving anyway, why not start the packing process early, and at the same time, get rid of all those treasures you can temporarily do without? Label each box carefully so you can find things easily later.

You want people to see your home as "theirs." When a room is too full, prospective buyers see all the "stuff" and don't necessarily see the potential of the house. One man had eight bright scatter rugs in the living room on top of the carpet. When you walked into the room, your eyes focused on these mats and not on the fabulous large window, high ceiling, gas fireplace, well-kept deck, and beautiful garden.

At times we have actually rented a storage locker for the excess items to make the house look more spacious.

THINGS TO ADDRESS INSIDE THE HOUSE

Things to do — general

- Remove all wallpaper if possible (neutral decor is important).
- Give a fresh coat of paint to high-wear areas such as doors, door frames, and around windows.
- Paint rooms that have undesirable colors in neutral tones if your realtor feels it's important.
- Paint ceilings that are stained. If you have had a water leak and fixed it, but the stains remain, people will wonder if there's still a problem.
- Remove old carpets if there is hardwood under them. Refinish if necessary. This "hidden treasure" can add value to your home.
- Make sure all appliances are in working condition.
- Make sure the water heater, air conditioning unit, and furnace are working properly.
- Repair loose handrails.

- Repair all inoperative electrical outlets or light switches.
- Make sure all smoke detectors and burglar alarm systems are in working condition.
- Remove cat litter, pet bedding, etc. (One client had several dogs and found a temporary home for them.)
- Eliminate all odors, e.g., smoke, dog, cat, etc. A fresh, clean smell always leaves a good impression. Use air fresheners or vanilla candles sparingly.
- Give the house a good cleaning. If you are hiring someone to do it, make a specific list of the things you want done.
- Remove all spider webs and dust.
- Wash the windows.
- Other ideas

Entrance
Picture the new owner welcoming guests in the front hall.

- Is it welcoming?
- Does the entrance look fresh or is a touch-up needed?
- Is the light fixture working? Is the bulb bright enough?
- Is it overcrowded with furniture?
- Is there clutter in the area (including your shoes)?
- Does the closet look overcrowded with the door open? If so, remove out-of-season clothing. Tidy the items on the shelf and on the floor.
- Other ideas

Living room

- Remove clutter and personal photos. Depersonalizing a home is meant to help the prospective buyers picture the house as "their home" with their belongings in it. As mentioned earlier, you can box and label items to move to your new home.
- Accentuate whatever is the major selling feature of the living room (a large window, a fireplace, a cozy feeling, an area that's great for entertaining, a bookcase, a piano).
- Paint walls with a neutral color.
- Rearrange the furniture (although the furniture arrangement may have worked for you, rearranging furniture can enhance the appearance of a room). The agent or stager might have some excellent suggestions.

- Make sure the windows, floors, walls, and furniture are clean.
- Remove dust from picture frames and lampshades.
- Clean fireplace if needed.
- Other ideas

Dining room

- Remove any furniture that makes the room look overcrowded.
- Remove personal items such as photos and clutter.
- If there is a china cabinet, remove some items if it looks crowded.
- If the table is worn, put a clean tablecloth on it.
- Put away any items of great value (e.g., sterling silver).
- Set the table or put fresh flowers or candles on it.
- Other ideas

Kitchen

This is a very important room. You can't change the size or shape of the room but you can make it show well. If the kitchen looks really worn, are there things that you could do to upgrade it, such as a fresh coat of paint, new cabinets, new flooring, new cabinet handles. Talk with your realtor to see what would be a worthwhile investment. Buyers need to see lots of counter space so they can visualize how they will use it. If the counters are full of "stuff," it's a difficult thing to do. Try to have the counters as empty as possible. More suggestions:

- Remove unused items from the cupboards (box and label the things you want to keep). Now put many of the things that have been on the counters in an accessible spot in the cupboards.
- Use the highest wattage light bulbs allowable to make the room as bright as possible.
- Make sure the appliances are clean and working well.
- Check vents and exhaust fans. Clean or replace if necessary.
- Clean the sink and polish the faucets. If the faucets are old or dripping, fix or replace them.
- Wash floor, countertops, and the fronts of the cupboards.
- Make sure the table, if there is one, looks clean, neat, and tidy. Remove a leaf to make the room feel larger.

- Put a tablecloth on the table if it is worn.
- Remove garbage regularly to eliminate odors.
- Make sure there are no strong odors coming from the fridge.
- Other ideas

Bathrooms

Again, this is an area that can help sell a house. You can't easily change the size but you need to make it look the best possible.

- Clean everything. Make sure there is no mold or mildew. If necessary, remove wallpaper and give the room a fresh coat of neutral paint.
- Invest in new towels. The majority of people we see have old, worn towels. For twenty dollars, towels can really help the appearance of a bathroom.
- Replace the shower curtain, if necessary. If there are glass doors, make sure they are clean.
- Make sure your Jacuzzi tub, if you have one, is working properly.
- Caulk or grout tub/shower if necessary.
- Replace or fix faucets if old or dripping.
- Replace mirror if damaged.
- Keep counters as empty as possible.
- Use the brightest light bulbs allowable. Clean the light fixtures.
- Make sure the exhaust fan is working and quiet. New ones cost little and are easily installed.
- Organize cabinets so they look tidy and uncrowded.
- Remove garbage.
- Put out a fresh bar of soap and a guest hand towel on the counter.
- As mentioned earlier, a vanilla candle or mild deodorizer can make the room smell fresher (strong deodorizers can be a turnoff).
- Other ideas

Bedrooms

- Remove excess furniture to make the rooms look as spacious as possible.
- Arrange furniture to give a good first impression.

- Remove any clutter.
- Remove all personal items.
- Make the bed look attractive even if you need to buy a new comforter.
- Dust and polish the furniture and clean mirrors.
- Organize closets to make them look spacious and tidy. Put out-of-season clothing away, if necessary.
- Install shelving to accommodate overflowing items.
- Other ideas

Laundry area

- Make sure appliances are working and clean.
- Discard cleaning products you no longer use.
- Make the area look tidy and bright.
- Put laundry away.
- Other ideas

Basement

When people are thinking of moving, we often suggest that they start in the basement. Frequently it contains lots of broken or outdated items. We see hundreds of plastic margarine containers, broken light fixtures, even broken broom handles in many basements. We also see fabulous antiques like pine blanket boxes and Limoges china! Call an antique dealer and/or charity and see what they might take.

Perhaps a local teenager can work with you. Put out items with your trash if you can. If not, make a trip to landfill or call a business that will remove junk for a fee.

TIP: If there is a usable basement window, a lot of smaller items can exit quickly, eliminating many trips up the stairs! More suggestions:

- Use a dehumidifier if it's damp or musty.
- Clean the floor; paint it if needed.
- Remove all spider webs.
- Remove or replace torn or dirty curtains.
- Other ideas

Garage

· Make sure the door opener is working.
· Get rid of items that won't be moving with you (sometimes first-time buyers are happy to have a lawnmower, hose, rake, shovel, garbage pails . . . if you won't be needing them).
· Sweep or hose down the garage.
· Replace light bulbs if necessary.
· Remove or replace dirty or torn curtains.
· Get rid of all spider webs.
· Make the garage look spacious and tidy so a buyer can visualize using it.
· Other ideas

Frequently homes with furniture show better than homes that are empty. Some homes need so much work they are sold "as is." We saw a house that needed new shingles, paint, new windows, an updated kitchen, a new bathroom, furnace, and back porch sell reasonably quickly. Some may even be a "tear-down" and sell for land value only. Any property will sell when it is priced properly. Discuss options with your realtor.

SHOULD YOU USE A REALTOR?

Some people want to sell their homes on their own. Consider the following:

· Do you know how to price the home? If your price it too high, you will attract the wrong buyers with higher expectations. If it is priced too low, you can lose money.
· Are you concerned about your personal security?
· Do you want to "show" your own home? It is hard to be impartial about things that you feel are important, yet might not matter to a prospective buyer. Will you take it personally if they criticize your home?
· Some buyers might not be comfortable dealing directly with an owner.
· What will advertising cost?
· Are you able to advertise as effectively as a realtor?

- Will you give too much information and disclose your motivation?
- How will you know you have a qualified buyer with approved financing?
- Are you able to negotiate what isn't to be included in the sale?
- Do you understand the legal ramifications of selling a home? Can you handle legal contracts and disputes with buyers?
- Do you have a lawyer who can check out the contract? What is the cost?
- Do you need a home inspector?
- Can you deal with building inspection issues and possible re-negotiations?
- Do you need a termite inspector? (It depends on the climate you live in.)

WARNING TO FAMILIES AND SENIORS

When the "For Sale" sign goes up, beware of opportunists looking to get things for nothing or pay as little as possible. At times people suddenly become "friendly" and ask what is going to happen to your car or the "stuff" you can't bring with you. We've also heard of that "nice" man coming to the door and paying $200 for all the family silver. We suggest that our seniors give a standard reply: "Our lawyer is looking after everything."

CHAPTER 10

Downsizing—
Making It Happen

TWO SONS WERE URGING their mom to make quick decisions on things she would like to keep and bring to her new home. You could literally see the anxiety building up in her eyes and facial expressions. Glaring at her boys, she took a deep breath and snapped, "What if I had to decide between the two of you?" The sons got the message, backed off, and took a more patient attitude toward their mom's "lifetime treasures."

The majority of people are extremely anxious about what to do with their "stuff." Women frequently get bogged down because so many things have precious memories and they simply can't keep everything They can usually tell you a story about each item and are reluctant to part with any of them. Children, on the other hand, tend to have more of a simplistic agenda that comes to a screaming halt when Mom starts sorting her treasures, trying to decide what to bring.

Occasionally men will simply say, "Shovel it out and send me the bill!"

One gentleman had five university degrees and discarded all of the diplomas. He said, "They are no use to me now." Some men, on the other hand, do have difficulty dealing with memorabilia and other manly treasures.

FIVE STEPS IN DOWNSIZING

1. What to keep
2. What to give to family or friends
3. What to sell
4. What to donate
5. What to discard

1. WHAT TO KEEP

Although we encourage each person to keep what is *really* important, the nature of downsizing dictates that some tough decisions need to be made. We have seen some people keep way too much, making it a very long, expensive, and frustrating experience for everyone on moving day as they tried to shoehorn it all in.

An important first step in deciding what to keep is to take a careful look at the new residence and see what will fit. Once there is an understanding of the available space, it will help with many critical decisions.

Often people make a list of what to keep. This is a great start, but over the years we've found a much more effective process that provides visual reminders as well as a certain level of comfort: COLORED REMOVABLE DOTS. They are a useful tool for anyone who is downsizing. Placing the color-coded dots on things to keep provides a level of reassurance to people while reducing the risk of discarding the "treasures." For those with memory loss, the dots are a great comfort. They are less confused when they can look around a room and quickly identify what will be coming with them.

TIP: Try to identify the items you are keeping *before* the extended family arrives to see what they would like. If there is a green dot, the item is not negotiable and moves with you or your senior.

Judy is a mom and a grandma. If one of our children were to say, "I've always loved that picture," she would give it to him or her even if it were the item she valued most and had planned to bring with her. Her dot on it says, "NO!" before anyone even asks.

Later, family members can use varicolored stickers to identify what will be given to others, sold, or donated to charities. The last decision is easy: discard the rest! The dots provide clarification for family members and loved ones that can help prevent misunderstandings or conflicts. Remember, the last thing anyone needs during this time is unnecessary "problems."

If you are relocating far away, check out the cost of moving your furniture. Some people move only their "treasures" and purchase new furniture when they arrive, because moving costs would be prohibitive. Some buy retirement homes that are already furnished and replace the items they don't like. Perhaps the surplus can be sold or simply given away. *Adult children*: If you are working with parents, try to make them feel that they have at least some control in the decision-making process. Help them by saying something like, "There is room for three chairs. Which three would you like to bring?" Narrowing down the decisions for them is helpful, but make sure it is based on an understanding of what is really important to them. One lady wanted to bring an old curio cabinet. She explained that she had spent a lot of time in her grandmother's home as a child and this antique was a big part of her wonderful memories there. We made room for it.

A lady wanted to bring her bed and her sofa-bed to a single room so her sister could visit once or twice a year. Her elderly brothers were trying to convince her to leave the sofa-bed, based on the limited space she was moving to. As the family looked on with furrowed brows, Judy said, "The sofa-bed will fit . . . OR you could bring your china cabinet. Of course if you brought the cabinet, you could also bring some notepaper and your beautiful china cups and saucers, as well as your knick-knacks . . ."

"I'll bring my china cabinet," she declared with a distinct look of satisfaction. (This is an example of a non-confrontational approach especially for people with Alzheimer's that allows them to participate and, in some cases, feel they are still 100 percent in charge.)

This is not an easy move for seniors. Familiar, sentimental belongings are very important in making the new residence feel more comfortable. Remember, "Home is where your stuff is." Also, whether you are young or old, if you get rid of something sentimental or valuable, you usually can't get it back.

Bring the things that are important to you or your parent. If the daily routine involves taking a NAP ON THE SOFA, see if you can "work it in." If BOOKS are important, bring a bookcase, a comfortable chair, and a good reading lamp. When GARDENING is important, bring some plants, a watering can, and even some fertilizer. Some places are receptive to having tenants help with the gardening. Some seniors' residences have raised flower boxes and encourage the "gardeners" to look after the flowers. On one occasion, after setting up a new residence, we were excited to show it to our client. Only one problem. We couldn't find her or her daughter anywhere. It turned out they had made their way up to the rooftop garden and were busy planting flowers! If CRAFTS are enjoyed bring wool, material, or even a sewing machine. If GRANDCHILDREN will be visiting, bring a few books, puzzles, cards, or maybe a game or two. We've found it is a great way to enjoy the visit and encourage the grandkids to return again and again. If BRIDGE is a favorite pastime, bring cards and possibly a card table. Some women invite friends and serve simple refreshments. If a COMPUTER is used, be sure to make room for it or buy a laptop, as it would take up much less space.

Hints and tips

Clothing

Judy was having great difficulty sorting through and discarding some of her own clothes and realized that many women, especially seniors, have trouble parting with years of accumulated clothing. She has since come to appreciate that it's easier to get rid of excess clothing when you know others will benefit. In our city there is a clothes-lending service for women who need something special to wear to a job interview. There are also battered women, refugees, nursing homes, street people, and charities like the Salvation Army that can use them.

Some women think their clothing can be sold, but unless they are new or retro and clean, it's not an option. Diplomatically say, "It's not saleable, but it's usable." We have had a few outfits from the forties and fifties that were desirable, especially ones with a New York, London, or Paris label. Here are some guidelines to help you make good, quick decisions on clothing:

Start by discarding clothing that is badly soiled, frayed, or needs major repairs. If the move is to a residence, avoid bringing items that need dry cleaning. Some coats may still be in excellent condition but are too heavy to wear comfortably. Give them away! Some zippers and some buttons are too difficult to use, and some sweaters don't fit over heads easily. Out they go!

Women sometimes keep clothes that are too small or too large hoping to "grow" or "shrink" into them. Be realistic and don't keep a size 10 when a size 14 is being worn.

As you sort through clothes, focus on what to keep. Choose clothing that makes one feel good about oneself. What are favorite colors? What colors are disliked? If you're working with your mom, you could take her shopping or bring three or four outfits home and let her choose a favorite one. Consider putting one of the others aside for a gift.

We put "keepers" to one side of the cupboard and leave the rest on the other side for the moment. It's quick and not as tiring as having to make a decision on each item. Passing over an item, think or say something like, "That is hard to put on now." Or, "Mom, you look so much prettier in this one . . . You want to look your best."

Avoid saying things like, "I can't believe you still have that old thing!"

Shoes

Often seniors are limited when it comes to choosing shoes. They need something comfortable, yet safe. Some can wear a small heel and a few can still wear a high heel. This helps make sorting easier.

We moved a special lady many years ago. She'd had a stroke and was confined to a wheelchair, so she and her husband moved to a continuing care facility. She discarded boxes and boxes of stiletto heels but kept one "memory" pair. A year later, her husband phoned to tell us her health had greatly improved and they were moving to a condo. They gave us the keys to both places and said, "We're taking the train for a holiday and will be back in three days. Move us while we're away." She walked out of the residence in her stiletto heels! Often this "shoe" story gives hope to people who have had a stroke.

Furniture for boomers

Rooms in adult bungalows, condos, apartments, and residences usually will not accommodate large sofas, big dining room tables, and king-sized bedroom sets. If *one* of these items is very important, we encourage you to choose a place that is large enough to accommodate it.

We've noticed baby boomers buying lots of new furniture for their new home. At first we thought, "Why discard nice things?" Then we remembered that when we downsized to a much smaller home, that's exactly what we did. Have a look at the new place and take some measurements. At times a room will accommodate a piece of furniture if you remove a large window, or carry the piece up several flights of stairs because it will not fit in the elevator. Otherwise it might be impossible to get it into the new residence.

There are times when shopping for smaller furniture is necessary. Furniture on a scale that's more appropriate is needed. Our large furniture wouldn't fit, so we bought a smaller sofa and tables. If you are purchasing new furniture, remember that too many colors in a small space will make the area look cluttered. Instead, use one color and play with different shades. You can use accent pieces of another color.

Furniture for seniors

When choosing a chair, take the one that is easy to get in and out of. If it's coming from the present residence, it is probably a favorite one. If purchasing new, make sure the person who will be using it actually tries it before buying it. Some people have long legs and some have short ones. Make sure that feet can touch the floor, and that it's comfortable to sit in.

Choose a dresser that is solid and easy to open. If there is any doubt, say, "Show me how easily you can open the drawers."

When working with a parent or a partner, be sensitive as to what they've been talking about. Try not to argue with them but repeat what they have said; e.g., "You've mentioned several times lately that you would like a dining room set that is a lighter color. Would you like to go looking on Saturday morning?" Use their words to open the door to selling, donating, or disposing of an item or purchasing something new.

Some relatives can overreact to change. A daughter was quite hurt when she bought a new lampshade for her dad, and he said, "I don't want a new one!"

Before showing him the lampshade, she could have said, "Dad, you asked me to buy a white lampshade. Here is what you asked for."

An elderly lady wanted to save her money in order to have something to leave her children, so she was hesitant about spending money on herself. At times, quality of life diminishes because of this strong desire. We always told Doug's mom the money she had was hers. We encouraged her to spend it. We also let her know that if she needed financial help, we would always be there to help her.

On the other hand, one of our seniors put up with the same sofa for fifty years. Her husband saved and saved and saved. After he had died, she announced, "I'm going shopping for new furniture!"

Avoid saying things like, "Your sofa is disgusting. It is worn and dirty." Remember, they don't see as well as they used to, their sense of smell is diminished, and if they have gone through the Depression or a recession, they can be very hesitant about spending money.

Instead, be positive. "Mom, that sofa has served you very well. I can't believe it's lasted this long, but it's time to replace it. Perhaps you'd like a love seat for your new home. It would also take up less space."

Sometimes "trading" is an option. You could say, "Mom, you have always admired my dining room set. It's quite a bit smaller than yours. Would you like to trade? Mine would fit better in your new apartment and I do have room for yours!"

You could give your parents a gift certificate from a furniture store and encourage them to use it toward something for their new home.

If your parent is considering doing some room arrangements that don't make sense, don't say, "That is ridiculous!" Instead, ask why he wants to do it that way.

We live in a small waterfront home. Our bedroom contains a large bed and two night tables. There is no dresser. WHY? No room! However, our bedroom faces the river and the larger bedroom in our home only faces the road. We wanted to wake up and see the water and the distant mountains and not see and hear the traffic.

Several times clients who were moving to a two-room suite have told us to put one of the beds in the living room. Why? Neither of them would have a good night's sleep if they slept in the same room. There are some fabulous room dividers or screens that are helpful in this situation.

2. WHAT TO GIVE TO FAMILY AND FRIENDS (BOOMERS OR SENIORS)

CAUTION! Lots of wisdom and understanding required here.

Is anything to be given to family or friends? "Stuff" can bring out the worst in some people. It can be a very challenging time for some families. We saw two brothers feuding over their father's three-hundred-dollar power tool. Perhaps the parent should have just sold it and divided the money or bought a second one for his other son. At times people want items just because they feel they can sell them for a lot of money. A suggestion is to put a monetary value on the items to help all see the fairness or unfairness of who is taking what. If need be, have art and other large dollar items appraised. Family peace is worth the fee. Some parents sell everything they can't bring with them without discussing it with their children, which upsets their family. In spite of this, money can be divided more equitably than material things.

Often a child wants a memento that is worth little. When Doug's mom gave up her home, Doug only wanted the old white enamel kitchen table. When he was a young child, the doctor came to the house and removed his tonsils as he lay on that table! It became a useful addition to his workshop.

At times, gifts such as a handcrafted item or an original piece of art can be returned to the giver, if he/she would like it back.

Some families take turns choosing an item they would like from the "what-to-gives." Each family member has a turn, then they go through the process over and over until all items are gone.

All in all, you're probably beginning to realize that the actual move is not the only stressful part of downsizing!

A positive outcome!

We have seen several parents who had been alienated from their children for many years reconcile during this time. Parents sent letters to their children saying that they were selling the house and wondered if there was anything they would like from the home. In these cases, "stuff" broke the ice and brought about renewed relationships.

Tips

We strongly encourage family members to keep the seniors' home somewhat intact until they actually move, especially the area that they spend most of their time in. Seeing their home in an empty or disorganized state can add to the stress they are already feeling. Judy remembers tears welling up in her eyes seeing an eighty-five-year-old alone and forlorn, sitting on one remaining chair in an otherwise empty room. Prior to the moving date, greedy family members had jumped the gun and grabbed everything their aunt wasn't taking with her.

It is equally important to leave sufficient time after the move to deal with what is left. This allows you (or your loved ones) time to take an additional lamp or end table to fill out the new home. It also gives them peace of mind knowing there is "a period of grace." If too much has been moved, it can be returned to the home and dispersed along with everything else.

We have emptied a large five-bedroom house in one day. All the decisions had been made and everything was effectively identified. The mover took items to deliver to the family. Next, the antique dealer and auctioneer arrived. A charity came a little later; then a load was taken to landfill. It is possible when you are organized and everything is coordinated efficiently.

3. WHAT TO SELL (BOOMERS OR SENIORS)

Now determine what items are saleable. Unfortunately, baby boomers as a demographic are typically downsizing, and the market for many things has become saturated, causing prices to be lower than they were several years ago. Many antique shops and consignment stores have closed because fewer people are interested in fine china, crystal, and silver. China needs to be carefully washed by hand, and today's society is more concerned about the lead in crystal. Silver is often sold by weight, and prices fluctuate. The market has reached the point where some items are no longer saleable, but merely giveaways.

Each city has reliable people with good names who will buy, consign, or auction the valuable and the not-so-valuable items. But beware! Like all other businesses, there are the usual "bad apples." Check out your choices with the Better Business Bureau or get a referral from someone who has been pleased with the service offered.

Ask lots of questions, such as:

· How do you establish prices for antiques and art?
· What commission do you charge?
· Do you charge to pack smaller items?
· Do you charge to transport all items?
· Do you charge for advertising?
· What happens if items don't sell?
· If unsold items are to be donated to a charity, do you charge for that service?

Having a sale

In the '60s, we lived in California, where so many things, like McDonald's and self-serve gas stations, got started. One morning a friend asked Doug to go to a garage sale. Doug said, "You have a garage, and I don't need one!" Returning to the East, we had the first garage sale in our community. It was a large charity sale and a great success. Of course, now garage sales are extremely common.

Sometimes, when the family, relatives, and neighbors have taken what they want, there is little of value left. Is it worth it to put in thirty to forty hours to get $200 *out of a sale*? If you feel it is worthwhile, an estate, contents, tag, or yard sale is another option available to you. Some people might shudder at the thought of a house contents sale, so this is not an option for everyone. The Internet, libraries, and bookstores are excellent sources for finding information on how to hold a sale, and what particular collectible items have sold for recently.

Frequently a lot of what has been accumulated over the years simply needs to be discarded. Dealing with the surplus is easier on elders' sensitivities after the move. After all, they have spent years collecting their "treasures," many of which have little cash value. Because of the sentiment attached to items, they might feel an item is worth hundreds of dollars when the reality is that a stranger might be willing to pay only five dollars.

If possible, don't show elders individual prices for items. Tell them what you got for several items rather than just for one of them. A collector's plate could have cost $60 and sold for $5, yet a Depression glass plate found in the basement might bring $40 rather than nothing. The total is $45, which is close to the expectation of what they would get for the two items. Often people are upset about the $5 item and unappreciative of the $40 item.

On the other hand, a lady remarked, "I've had that vase for years and I'm not really sure why — it's downright ugly! I don't care what you do with it!"

"Do you realize that vase is worth approximately $285?" Judy asked.

Guess what? It's now her favorite piece in the new home.

If you advertise, they will come. Helpful hints:

Advertise in the local paper, on-line, or on the community grocer's bulletin board.

Don't put the actual address in the ad. Say only, "Alder Street — watch for signs." Often no one is living in the home, and you don't want to alert thieves. It also keeps the opportunists and dealers at bay if you are setting up the night before.

Set a definite time. Say, "No sales before 8 a.m." Otherwise you could be inundated before you're ready.

Use a bold heading: "HOUSE CONTENTS SALE." It's worth the investment.

Be specific about items of value. Example:

"Excellent pine furniture, many power tools, original oak dining room set with 6 chairs, memorabilia, some collectibles . . . and much more!" (The tools keep the men busy while the women shop.)

Signs

Use wood or heavy cardboard and permanent markers. Make sure the sign and lettering are BIG enough that people can read them as they drive by. The sign should give: name of the sale, date and time, and street name (no number). Have signs on major roads near intersections at least the day before. Put signs on your street as well as connecting streets the morning of the sale. Use directional arrows on each one. Make sure the signs are sturdy and well fastened.

Set-up

Where feasible, price and leave items where they are. Considerable effort can be saved by pricing things where they are. It is easier on you if customers carry those sale items up the basement stairs. If you don't want them going through the whole house, limit the areas where they can go (e.g., main floor only, basement only).

Use as many tables as you can to display items more effectively. Borrow tables if you can.

If possible, have items priced. Price nothing under a dollar. Place several items in a clear plastic bag, staple it shut, and mark at $1.00-$5.00; or you could have a whole table of dollar items. Have change, paper, and a calculator on hand. Designate someone to sit at a table at the exit with a cash box to collect money from people as they leave. As the cash accumulates, remove it to a safe location. Take no checks.

If people want to go to a bank or ATM, tell them you will hold an item for twenty minutes, unless you know them or take a reasonable deposit. Another prospective buyer is usually willing to wait twenty minutes to see if the person has really bought the item that they have missed out on.

Sale day

If people arrive early, give out numbers starting an hour before you open. This allows you to be fair to the early birds and also to control the number of people entering at a time. Just before you open, inform the people waiting that prices are "as marked." No bargaining before noon. It's a sanity saver. If help is available and the weatherman cooperates, it doesn't hurt to put some of the bigger, pricier items out on the driveway. It says that your sale is substantial and not the typical "Let's-get-rid-of-the-kids'-toys" garage sale. Have someone available to monitor the customers around small valuable items, such as sterling silver.

STAY FOCUSED! We have seen some families agonizing over a table of small items that didn't sell. Your aim is to empty the house and keep your sanity as well. When you feel the time is right, remove items of value as well as those you would like to donate to specific charities. Then announce, "All remaining items are free. Take them away!" It is better that someone carries an item away rather than your having to pack it all up and dispose of it. Many charities have signs that say, "We take no garage sale leftovers."

The cleanup and removal of unsold items can take a lot of time. When the sale is over, take down the signs! **Have fun . . . Enjoy the people.**

4. WHAT TO DONATE (BOOMERS OR SENIORS)

Getting rid of long-time possessions can be a hard pill to swallow for many. There are two approaches. You can donate them to a worthwhile cause and get some satisfaction out of knowing that people are being helped. Or, if parting with the items is too much to handle at the time, consider renting some storage space for a short period of time.

Many items are still usable but not saleable. At times it is even difficult to give items away unless they are in good condition. Charitable organizations are often flooded with donations, so they have to be choosy about what they take. Several times we have sent decent, serviceable furniture to various charities and were told to take it to landfill. This has caused us to look elsewhere for solutions.

We now help battered women start over with items such as pots and pans and dishes, as well as pretty items to boost their self-esteem (such as clothing, flower vases, pictures, lamps, nice towels and sheets). Wool, fabric, etc., can go to a seniors' center. Recently we gave an enormous bag of wool to an elderly group of women who meet each week to knit for babies and street people. They were delighted!

- Food can go to the food bank, homeless shelters, etc.
  NOTE: Dispose of any outdated packaged or canned foods. If you wouldn't want your grandchildren to eat it, don't give it away.
- Wigs and some period clothing can be donated to the local theater group.
- Books can be given to a church or school for a fundraiser.
- Art supplies can go to a local art school or art center.
- Blankets, towels, soap, and shampoo can go to a shelter.

Recently we dropped off a large load of art books and art supplies to an art school. The people were ecstatic and gave us lots of hugs. Many would-be artists want to learn to paint and some can't afford to buy the supplies.

This is only a short list of some suggestions for donations. It is really satisfying to be able to help people, but more important, it's great to know that the belongings will be used and are helping others.

A client's granddaughter gave us some of her grandmother's size 3 clothing. We gave them to a tiny elderly lady who loved nice clothing and had a limited budget. She really appreciated them and the granddaughter was thrilled.

5. WHAT TO DISCARD (BOOMERS OR SENIORS)

REMEMBER, before you send a box to landfill, open it and check it carefully. You might have missed important papers such as deeds and wills. If you are going to discard papers, check for any personal information: name, address, phone number, account numbers, etc., and SHRED them. This is really important.

We have found sterling silver and chicken bones in the same container! Often money is found in books or rolled up in an old sock. Rings and safety deposit box keys might be hidden in old, chipped sugar bowls, between mattresses, or pinned inside old clothing.

Recently, working with masks and gloves, our workers took many boxes of fabric that mice had infested out of an attic under the ever-watchful eye of the elderly owner. We insisted on discarding it, although the man felt it was usable. He was unaware of the dangerous parvovirus carried by mice.

In the yard were two very rusted lawn chairs. We requested that the men put them in the trailer for landfill. The elderly man insisted that the items be removed from the trailer. He was not prepared to see anything go. We knew it was time to stop. If you are working with a parent, it is much easier to discuss what will be done; but have the senior occupied elsewhere the day that the residence is emptied.

NOTE: Check on restrictions for garbage, recyclables, and hazardous waste because each place is different. May you put furniture out with your garbage? Once we put 400 large, empty, plastic water jugs at the curb for recycling. We strung them together so that they could be untied easily when they were put in the truck. In our community, there is a hefty extra fee if you have any cardboard with your trash. On the other hand, we loaded a truck with four tons of paper from one house and, being environmentally correct, we delivered it all to the paper recycler. "Take it to landfill," was his reply.

At one time we could put out fifty bags of garbage. Now some cities charge for each bag. People purchase "tags" and each bag must have a tag attached to it. Some places simply restrict residents to one bag of trash a week! Often there are services available that will take a load of trash to landfill for a fee. Some businesses bag and remove the garbage, while others just remove it. Some recycle it, others don't. Charges are calculated by weight, volume, time, and/or dumping fee.

A diligent son-in-law gave us this list of some items they removed from the family house:

200 juice cans containing an estimated 100,000
rusty nails and screws
400 cans of paint, none full
4 tons of scrap wood
300 picture frames
50,000 loose photos
200 panes of glass
2,000 grocery store bags
1 ton of old pipes and other scrap metal
2,500 feet of old extension cords and other wiring
1,000 bits of rope, twine, and string
400 cups and saucers

Again, stay focused. Don't get caught up in that "Maybe I'm being wasteful" trap. Keep in mind the decisions made were by *a process of elimination!*

CHAPTER 11

The Move

A SON FLEW HOME to help his mom with her move. Although they had talked about it for several months, when he walked into the house he suddenly realized this was the LAST time he would be there. It was very emotional, as the home would be sold, and he could no longer return. There are many children who do not want their parent(s) to sell the family home and move. At times, a child's bedroom is the same way it was when the child left for college years before. Nothing has been removed! Nothing is changed! The move can be harder on some children than on their parents because the parents "know" it's time to move, and a child feels they should stay put. We have asked clients, "Are you still speaking?"

Our daughter refused to see our new home when we moved because we were selling her "childhood." She got married, moved to Hong Kong, and by the time she returned, all was well and visit she did! This experience helped prepare us for the roller coaster of emotions that our clients go through.

It is wise to arrange a move for a Tuesday, Wednesday, or Thursday if possible. Monday allows for a "get ready" day. Moving on a Friday means waiting until Monday to get help with unexpected problems because regular staff have the weekend off. This applies whether it be to a new bungalow or a retirement residence. Issues with phone, cable, plumbing, electrical issues, parking, security, etc., are best resolved before the weekend.

If your parent is moving to a retirement residence or nursing home, the dietitian, nurse, and activity director are there only during the week to answer questions. So a Friday move often means it will be Monday before special needs or requests can be implemented.

If possible, check out the new home a day or two before the move to make sure everything is ready. You don't want to arrive on moving day only to discover that a kitchen is not fully renovated as promised, or carpets still need cleaning. We've even found broken glass, dirty bathrooms, and multitudes of dead flies!

Try to be the first move of the day. It's the only time of day when you can be sure the movers will arrive on time, and it gives you longer to have the new home set up before the end of the day.

If you are ordering a new bed or sofa, have it delivered before the movers arrive. It is easier to see how the other furniture will fit in when the new pieces are already there. The men can also do some rearranging, if need be.

Many people like to transport important papers and valuable jewelry in the trunk of the family car, where it is locked and secure.

There are three ways to accomplish the move:
1. A senior move manager
2. A moving company
3. The family

1. A SENIOR MOVE MANAGER

Seniors who are moving often show signs of Relocation Stress Syndrome. Symptoms are exhaustion, sleep disturbance, anxiety, grief, depression, and disorientation. These symptoms are worse if there is dementia, frailty, poor physical health, or no proper support system. We often tell seniors that feeling exhausted even if they "do" nothing is quite common. It's part of the emotions of dealing with a lifetime of accumulations and memories. Senior Move Managers that are members of The National Association of Senior Move Managers (NASMM)[10] are trained to help elders and their families through these times.

A senior move manager will look after all aspects of a senior's move. This is great especially when family members are busy or live out of town. Remember, this can be a very upsetting time for many people. Many senior move managers help families navigate through the emotional times. This route allows the family time with the parent to tend to the personal and emotional needs she has. It is easier for your parent if you spend time with her and familiarize her with what's available in the building or neighborhood. You can introduce her to a "neighbor" or to staff members and sit with them and enjoy a cup of coffee.

Senior move managers check out the new residence, help choose the furniture that will fit, and make suggestions where it could be placed. They arrange for, and supervise, the movers and make every effort to ensure that the day runs as smoothly as possible. They oversee the packing, unpacking, and complete setup of the new home. They make up beds, plug in the lamps, hook up the computer and TV, organize the bathroom and kitchen(ette), and even hang the pictures. The familiar, treasured belongings help keep seniors in their comfort zone. The clients often walk into their new residence and say, "This feels just like home!"

Some senior move managers purchase linens or a TV, order the new phone, do change of address cards . . . They can arrange for the dispersal of remaining items to family members, friends, or charities. Move managers can also see that the home

---

10 Check the Internet for a group in your area.

is prepared for sale or arrange to have it cleaned for the new owners. Their fee will be for services provided.

2. MOVING COMPANY

A moving company will charge an hourly rate. They can do the packing and unpacking and reassemble the bed. (It still has to be made up.) They don't do the complete setups that move managers do. If they unpack, they usually don't put things away.

The more organized you are before the movers arrive, the smoother it will go, and the less it will cost. The elevator, if needed, should be booked well in advance. Plan where the heavy furniture will go. Carefully identify the items to be moved. Label the items to be left, delivered to a different address, or sent to storage. Don't bring too much. Shoehorning a lot of extras in takes much more time and the costs go up.

NOTE: If you do your own packing, most movers will not insure the items for breakage. If items are valuable, irreplaceable, or sentimental, move them yourself. We always remind our team that even a chipped mug that has come from a grandparent or a special friend is irreplaceable.

Ask the movers if there are any items they won't move. Many won't move liquids or plants. Both can be transported in plastic containers with tight-fitting lids. Lots of movers will not move mirrors unless they wrap or box them at an additional fee. Will they move the computer? Do you have to put it in its original box? Do they move food from the fridge or freezer?

Does the mover require you to empty all drawers? Usually we leave clothing in the drawers and put a towel over them so they won't move around too much when they have to be tipped to get in and out of elevators. It's hard enough to move, let alone having to wonder where specific items have been placed. On the other hand, a dresser can be damaged if it's old, heavy, and dried-out. In these cases we do empty the drawers. At times we remove the full drawers, number them to help us put them back in the right order, and carefully carry them to and from the truck. We actually transport them in the dresser while in the truck.

Most moving companies charge a minimum of three hours. Ask if their "start" time is when they leave the shop or when they arrive at the home. Some include a one-hour travel time in the three hours and others add the hour to the minimum. Most men are entitled to "breaks," but how many? Are you paying when they aren't working? Ask about this.

Schedule the move so that you arrive at the new residence at an acceptable time. If you have purchased the home, make sure you *will* have the key. We have arrived at one p.m. and waited with a full truck until the key arrived at four p.m. Remember that many inner-city elevators are not available when working people could be coming home for lunch. Retirement residences and nursing homes restrict elevator use at mealtimes. If the moving company does arrive at a mealtime, you will have to pay them for the hour that they have to sit and wait. Make sure you put your requests in writing. For example:

· Three wardrobes for the clothes
· Carpets covered
· Mattresses in mattress bags
· Mirrors boxed or wrapped
· Wooden furniture shrink-wrapped
· Other ideas

Although we have a Web site and are listed in the yellow pages, over 99 percent of our moves come from referrals from satisfied customers. So check with a friend or the place to which you are moving to see if they have a recommendation for you. Remember that the cheapest is not always the wisest choice. You want the move to be as stress-free as possible and you want experienced people who will be careful with all your possessions.

3. FAMILY

If you're not used to moving furniture, you can injure your back. If furniture is not padded or placed properly in the truck, it can be damaged. Professionals know how to move furniture quickly, efficiently, and carefully. They have a system that works and they are accustomed to working together. Once a "kindly person" insisted on helping Judy with a box. A piece of china got broken and had to be replaced at a cost of $400. Another time a well-intentioned helper caused Judy to trip and she ended up in the emergency ward needing stitches in her face. We firmly let the professionals do the moving.

Unless the move is to a nursing home or a small room and only a few things are being moved, we do not recommend this. Many times excellent friendships are strained over something that happens during a move. When family members gather, often from all over, they don't always get along or work well together. Trying to save money by renting your own truck can end up causing friction and stress for everyone. Longstanding, almost forgotten issues resurface. Frequently one child carries most of the responsibility for all the decision making. Sadly we have seen far too many families wind up almost at each others' throats over disagreements, bossiness, or plain old jealousy. (A seldom-seen relative arrives and takes over, leaving the child who had been the daily caregiver feeling snubbed, hurt, and angry.) Even families who know they are dysfunctional still feel they should "soldier through" a move because it's their duty. *All of this makes this time even more stressful for you or the person you are trying to help.*

TIPS ON PACKING

Some moving companies rent plastic moving containers for a few pennies a day. They are great for quick, easy packing, and you don't have to recycle the boxes and paper at the end of the move. The containers stack well and are weather resistant.

Box "necessities" together. One box could contain kitchen items that you will need right away. Another one could have bathroom items like soap, towel, toilet paper, and toothbrushes and toothpaste. Yet a third box could have linens for the beds.

Pack the phone, cable cord, extension cords, picture hooks, hammer, tape measure, and night light in a well-labeled box. It is also handy to have some glue with you in case a dried-out piece of furniture needs a little TLC. (We've seen legs fall off just by lifting a very old table that hasn't moved in twenty years.)

When you are packing, use unprinted newsprint, linens, or bubble wrap (with the bubble side out). Plates should be packed on the edge and glasses should be packed upside down. Don't put something heavy on top of something fragile. If you are using boxes, take the time to make sure each box is full. Top off the boxes with a towel or something soft. There is less chance of an item's being damaged from moving around when a box is full. Take the time to tape the boxes rather than folding in the top flaps. They will stack better and won't tip as easily. Label the boxes with as much detail as you can for easy identification later.

Pack liquids separately in a large plastic container. Make sure the lids are on securely and stand each item upright. Items like irons, kettles, and coffee makers often have small amounts of liquid in them that could damage a cardboard box. Don't move bleach. If the container leaks, many things can be damaged.

Order wardrobes for the hanging clothes. Movers sell, rent, or loan wardrobes, and they make the task much easier because clothes can stay on their hangers. If the weather is cold, remember to set aside the coats and hats that will be needed.

MOVING DAY

Whoever does the move, it is easier if not too many people are there. Someone can get hurt if a person is suddenly in front of the people carrying a heavy dresser. If your parent is moving, plan something special for him. Take him or send him out for breakfast with a friend or family member. Treat him to a hotel the night before the move if he has difficulty getting up early. Also, seeing his home being dismantled and boxes everywhere can be stressful. Some condos, apartments, and residences have furnished suites for rent. Make it fun! Make it special!

Know where the large pieces of furniture will go. Later you can move a chair or small table if necessary.

If you are working with elders, involve them in the final bit of setting up, e.g., where to put some of the pictures. At times we unpack their "treasures" and hand one at a time to them and let them "place" them where they want them. Although it may take longer with their help, as they start making small decisions, they are beginning to make it home.

If the move involves installing a medical aid like the "assist" pole,[11] have it professionally installed or see if the person in

---

11 An assist pole helps people get out of bed or off the toilet. There are two main types. One fits between the floor and the ceiling and needs to be professionally installed for safety reasons. The exact positioning of it is also very important, and often a specialist will show where it needs to be installed. It does not damage the floor or ceiling, but cannot be used where the ceilings are not solid. The other type is bolted to the floor and is about waist-high. When it is removed, the floor must be repaired.

charge of maintenance will install it. Many buildings have fake ceilings because plumbing or wiring needs to be accessible, and it is important to know that the equipment is secure and safe.

NOTE: Many years ago when we left our home of twenty-three years, we made a surprising yet reassuring discovery: As we walked through the house—with everything removed—it was no longer our home . . . Our home had left on the moving truck.

LIST FOR CHANGE OF ADDRESS

- Accountant
- Bank
- Cable
- Charities
- Chiropractor
- Credit cards
- Dentist(s)
- Doctor(s)
- Eye doctor
- Friends and family
- Gas company
- Groups or associations
- Homemaker
- Insurance agent
- Internet provider
- Investment company
- Lawyer
- Magazine subscriptions
- Newspaper
- Pensions
- Pharmacy
- Phone company
- Place of worship
- Post office
- Power
- Trust company
- Vehicle permit
- Veterinarian
- Other

CHAPTER 12

Some Thoughts
on Alzheimer's

FAMILY MEMBERS OFTEN don't recognize the early signs of Alzheimer's and get frustrated and angry at some of the subtle changes in behavior that slowly take over. As children, we often say things like, "Dad, I'm forgetful, too . . . You are just under a lot of stress." When a professional tells us that a parent has Alzheimer's, we tend to deny it and treat it lightly rather than address it and discuss the parent's fears with him. He can be terrified at the possibility of losing his mind. Yet we find ourselves calling the home and talking to a person who seems like someone else — not "him." This is a time for *more* support, not less. Your parent needs lots of reassurance you won't desert him or lock him away somewhere.

Although there is less stigma to Alzheimer's now than several years ago, many people have little knowledge of the disease.

Here is one example of what can happen as Alzheimer's sets in. The person can fretfully complain, "There was a stranger in my house last night." She wasn't hallucinating. She was seeing an old person in the mirror. Mentally she had slipped back in time — perhaps to when she was thirty or forty years old. That person in the mirror really was a stranger!

Another example: We took a relative out for lunch, and she went to the washroom. When she didn't return in a reasonable amount of time, Judy went looking for her. She was in the cubicle and couldn't get out. Judy crawled under the door and unlocked it so she could leave. (She couldn't remember how to open the door.)

Many doctors believe that we can slow down the progress of Alzheimer's (for most people) if they are diagnosed in the early stages and begin taking medication. Although current treatment does not prolong life, it usually gives a better quality of life. Some people have adverse reactions to the drugs and some don't. By the time you read this, they may have found a cure.

EARLY SIGNS OF ALZHEIMER'S

- Having difficulty finding words, finishing sentences, or remembering people's names when this hadn't been a problem before
- Repeating questions or statements
- Forgetfulness that is out of the ordinary
- Needing reminders to go shopping or take medications
- Needing help with usual daily activities
- Needing reminders to keep appointments for family occasions or holidays
- Becoming more irritable
- Changes in driving (getting lost, driving unsafely)
- Having difficulty balancing a checkbook
- Suddenly showing aggressive behavior
- Not participating in conversation like they used to
- Becoming sad or crying more often
- Consistently looking to someone to answer questions for them rather than answering them (a strong indicator)
- Finding things in unusual places (we have found garbage, new shoes, china, a growing plant, and unopened cans of food—all under the same kitchen sink)

If a significant number of the above apply, consult a doctor. For further information about early detection of Alzheimer's, visit *www.alzheimerinfo.ca.*

MOVING SOMEONE WITH ALZHEIMER'S

We have moved many people with Alzheimer's and have many reassuring and helpful experiences to share. We've discovered that an effective strategy for one person may not work with another. The following examples may give some useful insights as to what may or may not work for your loved one who needs to be moved to a care facility.

Bring familiar things like a favorite chair, desk, bookcase, TV. At times they can remember how to turn on an older TV and would have difficulty adapting to a new one. If books were special "friends," even if the senior no longer reads, they can still have some meaning. If a desk has been an important part of his daily life and there is room for it, bring this familiar piece of furniture. Bring lots of older familiar pictures. Try to make the new room "home."

For one gentleman, we put green dots on everything that was going with him and reminded him that "green means go." We arrived on moving day to discover that there were green dots on everything—each sock, each shoe, each handkerchief, each coin was carefully dotted, and he reminded us that "green is go." He had sent his son-in-law to the store to buy more green dots for him.

Now we use *two sizes* of dots. We put half-inch dots on the items to be moved, then gave the senior a package of smaller dots to use. It worked. This constant reminder kept him in his comfort zone.

We were moving an elder from the hospital to a secure unit in a nursing home. The door for the elevator looked like a bookcase when it was closed. When the elevator door was open, he stood threatening Judy with his cane. He wanted to get on the elevator and was simply told that it was on service but that it would be sent back for him. It was a reply he could accept. (Direct confrontation was avoided in favor of this alternative approach.) Later he recognized his entertainment unit when it arrived. Then he saw his chair and said, "That's mine." He had an enormous smile and said, "Thank you." (With many seniors, familiar belongings give contentment and make new surroundings feel more like home.)

We moved a couple into an Alzheimer's unit. She was on one floor with a small room and a single bed. He had a larger room with a double bed on a more restricted floor. They had been married over sixty years and weren't used to spending a night apart. Because we feel that every effort should be made to keep compatible couples together, we made a request for them to sleep together.

That night by nine o'clock she was asleep in her little bed and he was sitting in a little wooden chair contentedly watching her. Unfortunately an uninformed staff member came in and told him he had to leave. He went berserk and had to be sedated to calm him down. (Alzheimer's people have great difficulty with a small change in routine, let alone something of this magnitude.) Confrontation should always be avoided with Alzheimer's people. Don't say, "NO." It's better to sidestep as above or use a bit of humor. ("Let me check that out," "Maybe later," "Let's ask someone," are all examples of sidestepping.)

One hot July day, a client arrived at an Alzheimer's unit clad in a heavy winter coat that she insisted on wearing. We followed with her belongings. She met us at the door still warmly attired and informed us that she was going home. We asked her what her career had been. She had worked with the same pension department as Doug's dad. On asking if she knew him, she immediately exclaimed, "Of course I knew Slim." They had actually known each other quite well and we were able to talk about mutual acquaintances for two hours. She took off her coat and helped us prepare her room. (Talking about the past had calmed her and she was able to function.) People can often talk about things that happened in their forties, fifties, or sixties but cannot remember that they'd had a coffee ten minutes before.

Being able to carry on a conversation can have a calming effect on an Alzheimer's patient. Make a collage of their older pictures to help you or others carry on a conversation with them.

Doug's dad had no short-term memory. He thought Judy was his sister. We'd go for a sip of water and on our return he would say he hadn't seen us in months. We were thankful for caring staff that looked after him. Frequently we took him for a drive in the country or out for a donut. The conversation was always, "It's a nice day. It's a nice day. It's a nice day . . ." x 30! Judy usually had a cry before we drove away. (Here, patience is more than a virtue. It is a necessity!)

Judy became very attached to a lady she worked with. One day she really turned on Judy. The woman became very accusatory and distrustful and extremely offensive. Judy was devastated and didn't know what to do. She visited our "mentor" who managed a retirement residence and had a degree in gerontology. He said the magic words: "Don't take it personally — it's the disease." He added, "You look twenty years younger than when you walked in here." We strongly advise you to do likewise — don't take it personally.

Seniors will accuse children, friends, or neighbors of "taking things." In reality they have put items away and don't remember where they are. They also give things away or throw them out. If this is a concern, ask to borrow the family photos to make sure they don't go to landfill! If they ask about them reassure them that you have them and are still looking at them. Suggest that you put their valuable jewelry in a safety deposit box or safe. Again, if they ask about the items, tell them that they are safely stored. You can also leave a note that their treasures are in their safety deposit box. If they insist on moving valuable items, try to lock them away in a filing cabinet, a desk, or a china cabinet in their suite.

It is very hard when parents suddenly turn on you or start favoring other siblings with time and expensive gifts, especially when you have been the primary caregiver. Diseases and medications can affect people. You have to protect your parent and you have to be careful not to get bitter and allow relationships to be totally destroyed. Remember, *she* has the problem—not you! She is no longer the parent you once knew.

Be cautious of strangers taking advantage of your parent.

While we were preparing to move one lady (not knowing she had some memory loss), some people arrived at the door to pick up the refrigerator she had given them. Our suspicious questioning so upset our client that we relented and let them have it. Later we determined that she had met these new "friends" at a bus stop a few days earlier and had offered it to them. Her lawyer then informed us that the refrigerator was to have been included in the sale of the house! We now get a list of inclusions from the lawyer or realtor.

We have seen several cases where "strangers" or distant relatives have befriended a senior and over time have brainwashed and alienated mothers from children living far away to the point where they actually disowned a child. In each case, the parent had dementia. Guess who took control of the finances?

Dealing with Alzheimer's patients is never easy. Take heart. You are not alone. You're following in the footsteps of many others before you. See if there is an Alzheimer's support group in your neighborhood.

CHAPTER 13

Settling In

BOOMERS

If people ask to help, be specific as to how they can. Some suggestions:

- Provide supper.
- Look after pet.
- Vacuum before the movers arrive.
- Meet phone or cable service at new residence.
- Line shelves with fresh paper.
- Help unpack the kitchen.
- Hang drapes.
- Other

Once the furniture is placed, we usually get the bed(s) made up first. If necessary, find a cover for the bedroom window so you can retire quickly when ready.

Next, unpack the kitchen and bathroom necessities. You want to be able to make a cup of coffee or a cool drink and have a relaxing bath or a shower.

Put some of the boxes that you don't need to unpack yet out of sight. It's helpful if there's at least one place that is uncluttered and peaceful, so try to bring some order to at least one place. If it's been a long day, everything else can wait until the next day.

ASSISTANCE FOR SENIORS

If possible, have a meal with your loved one in her new home the day of the move. It doesn't matter if you go to the dining room, or have a pizza in her suite. You're trying to state that this is her home and she can still entertain.

Mealtime is very important for seniors. Ask the manager to seat Mom or Dad with someone compatible. It's hard to be interested in world affairs or business and sit beside someone who only talks about her bad health or isn't even able to carry on a conversation. We've seen many strong relationships develop between seniors in residences. In one case, a young worker was befriended by an eighty-year-old man. When the gentleman died, the young man did the eulogy for his friend. It was amazing!

Maintaining outside contact is important. Encourage the elder to invite friends or neighbors for tea or a meal. If they have played bridge together, ask the group to come one afternoon. A few months ago, we moved a lady who was turning one hundred. A young professional woman about forty years old arrived, and Judy asked her if she was a granddaughter. "No," she responded, "I'm her friend. I knew that she was moving today so I took time off work to be with her." We watched and listened to them as they talked about birds, cats, and gardening.

Many people take six months to fully adjust to life in a residence. If they have friends in the building, or make friends easily, and are interested in other people, the transition is easier. On the other hand, if they have had a major loss in their life or are in constant pain, it is harder to make the adjustment.

We encourage seniors to stay active and continue learning new things. It is important that their life still feels worthwhile. Several clients in their eighties have written and published their first books. In fact, we'd been toying with writing this book for seven years, and it was an eighty-six-year-old lady who was the catalyst for us to get at it. We had moved and settled her and were emptying her apartment. A large envelope of organized papers surfaced and we felt that it was important to ask her if she wanted it.

"Yes," was her reply. "It's my manuscript, and my publisher said to keep it."

We asked her how much she had paid and how many copies she needed to order to get it published.

"Nothing!" was her reply. "They published my book!"

That was the motivation and challenge for us to get serious and start writing this book.

We asked a lady in her nineties what new thing she was going to do in her new residence. She replied, "I'm going to learn to play pool!" Several years later, we saw her and asked how the pool was going. She replied, "I'm in disgrace. I beat the minister."

A gentleman got his first computer at ninety. He's now ninety-seven and has his third one. Research shows that keeping your mind active helps fend off depression and dementia. If a ninety-year-old can learn how to send e-mails, then a seventy-year-old can, if desired.

One senior recorded her first musical CD.

When we moved a ninety-year-old lady to a retirement residence, we jokingly asked her, "When are you going to be in supervising the kitchen?" Within a week, she was showing the staff how to make muffins for diabetics!

Give your parents time to make new relationships. Don't be there every day after they move in. Whatever pattern you set at the start is what they will expect. If you have been very close, you will find it hard not to go every day. If you need to, send your spouse or a grandchild with "something." Set aside a regular visiting time that will work for everyone. It could be a time for shopping, appointments, lunch, theater, or dinner at your home. Seniors do best with routines (the first Sunday of the month, every second Tuesday . . .).

Many children refuse to go away for a holiday when a parent is in a retirement residence or nursing home. It actually is a good time to go away, as the parent is well cared for; if an emergency occurred and you had to come home, you could. The doctor of a friend's mother told her that her mom had just weeks to live. Well, that was over three years ago, and Mom keeps getting better, even with the big "C."

Many parents play havoc with their children's emotions. A friend's mother used to call her at all hours and say, "I wish you were dead!" Finally the daughter put call block on her phone. She visits and talks with her mom on her terms. Call display is also handy.

Having seen a client quite happy at a residence, we called the son long-distance to tell him. The son responded, "My dad calls me every day to tell me how upset he is and how it's all my fault!"

We have learned from the many seniors we have worked with that mental games and "guilt trips" can be quite common. For your own peace of mind, remember: Happiness is a choice — a choice only they can make.

CELEBRATING THE HOLIDAYS

Include your loved ones in the celebrations if possible. They can choose gifts from a catalog with your guidance. Often they will give a gift of cash. Take them shopping or buy some cards for them to sign to include with their gift.

Reminisce about other festive occasions. You could talk about the special cakes they made or bought and how loved you felt because of their effort and care. Look at albums from past holidays. Small decorations for their suite can help them get into the spirit of the holiday. Bring some homemade treats for them to enjoy and share with others. Join them for dinner or ask several family members to come to the family dining room for a meal.

If possible, bring your loved ones to your home. At times seniors have difficulty handling crowds and lots of activity and noise. If you're having a crowd, have a quiet corner or room where they can go to rest if needed.

Holidays are very emotional times for lots of people. It's even harder when you feel useless. Many years ago Judy was in a bad car accident. She could do nothing — not even reach over for a sip of water. It really prepared her for working with seniors. When people have been very active and involved in life and suddenly have a stroke, it's FRUSTRATING. They want to do things and simply can't. Acknowledge their limitations and frustrations and try to encourage them and let them know that you're glad they are still a part of your life.

It is a time when you can listen to them and learn a lot about your family. Many parents were very private people. At times they went off to war and returned "changed"; their experiences changed them and it affected their relationships, yet often they never discussed them. Recently, I worked with a man who had lost both his legs. He told me how lucky he was and I just listened. I kept thinking, how could he be "lucky"? Well, he lost both legs jumping out of a plane, but both his friends lost their lives. He is at least alive to tell about it!

Frequently we're asked what makes the difference between being happy or unhappy when you're "old." From what we have seen, it seems to be the focus — self or others. We often say, "The fact is, you can't change some things, but you can try and make a difference where you are. Make the best of the time you have."

CHAPTER 14

Companionship

SEVERAL YEARS AGO, we moved a couple in their nineties. Both were quite small, and he walked with a cane. One day she remarked, "He's very frail in the daytime, but boy, is he good at night!" Judy's shocked response was, "Ohhhh . . . how long have you been married?"

She replied, "We're not married, dear."

"How long have you been together?"

"Thirty-seven years. If I married him, I'd lose my pension."

About ten days later, we were back at their condo. We had just finished emptying it and saying our goodbyes when Doug quipped, "Now you two be good."

She replied, "Douglas, we have to. You took the beds!"

Neither of us were prepared for what we heard. Yet, since then, we have moved many couples in their eighties who are "getting together." Some get married and some don't. Some share a bedroom and some don't. Some keep their own residences and spend weekends and holidays together. Even with Viagra, the

younger generations can't believe that seniors can still be "interested." They are! **We strongly recommend** that in the event of a late marriage, both seniors see their lawyers and look at cohabitation agreements or prenuptial contracts. (This could avoid future misunderstandings and help ease both families' concerns.) They should also agree in writing as to the financial commitments that they are making.

Judy's dad remarried several years ago. She still remembers, "I was unhappy and judgmental at the time." Even now, it's difficult to put into words how she felt. Since we've been in this business, our attitude and outlook have changed. We now see the loneliness that so many seniors endure.

We've heard widows say, "Treasure your husband." "You don't know how lucky you are." "Your life can change in a minute." "I'm so very lonely." "It's hard to always eat alone."

A major problem with growing old is loneliness. When a spouse dies, suddenly the home seems so very empty. The days and nights are very long, so if by chance the person meets someone, doesn't he or she have the right to companionship?

ADDITIONAL CONSIDERATIONS

· Should the couple keep their finances separate and divide the expenses between them?
· How do they divide expenses?
· Should one partner become mentally incompetent, who will speak for them or protect their interests (their partner or a child)?
· Whom does the house belong to?
· Can the surviving partner live in the house as long as he/she lives?
· What if he/she finds another partner?
· Who pays the expenses — the surviving partner or the estate?
· If the surviving partner wants to sell the house, can he/she live off any of the proceeds, or does the money get dispersed?

Encourage your parent to *see a lawyer!* We see major problems in families when it comes to money or possessions.

NOTE: We are not here to give legal advice. We are simply sharing some of the things that we have heard and seen in order to provide you with things to think about and help you to make informed decisions.

Parents have often had to adjust to their children's misadventures and may have sacrificed so that their children could go to college, only to see them quit before graduating.

A child could arrive home and lay one or several of the following surprises on a parent:

"You're going to be a grandma!"
"I failed my year."
"You'll never have my grandchildren. I'm gay."
"I'm in jail."
"I was caught drinking and driving."
"You have never loved me and I don't love you."
"I'm deep in debt."
"I've joined the army and I'm going off to war."
"I wrecked the car."
"I'm an addict."
And so on . . .

Most parents are just that — PARENTS. They love their children and although they are quite disappointed, they will do what they can to help. They might not always do the right thing, or what you think is right, but at least they attempt to help. Now it can be your turn to allow them some help and companionship in their later years!

Most parents want to provide something for their children through their wills, but do remember that this is their money, not yours.

CHAPTER 15

Some Thoughts
on Gifts for Seniors

MOST PEOPLE ENJOY receiving gifts. Yet as people get older, it seems harder to buy for them, especially with limited living space. Seniors often say, "Don't buy me anything. There's nothing I need." Well, we've discovered that is not necessarily the truth. There are lots of things seniors need, but a change in thinking is necessary.

As previously mentioned, what seniors want and need most of all is your TIME, and sometimes the hardest thing to find is TIME, especially when you feel that it's a "duty" thing.

Some ideas:

- Buy her a new outfit ("And I'll take you shopping on Tuesday to get it!") (Outings give seniors a break from routine.)
- Give him a handwritten invitation for lunch out next Sunday.
- Pick him up and take him to his place of worship.
- Take her to a movie or some live entertainment.
- Take her for a manicure.
- Pick up four or five bathrobes and let him choose one (return the others).
- Make a collage of people or things that are important to her. (This can be enjoyed daily.)
- Hire a photographer to take a family portrait with him (frame it and display it).
- Invite her for a visit to your home to show you how to make a special recipe (e.g., pie, jam, soup . . .).
- Ask him to help you write or record some of his memories and family information for the next generation before they are lost forever (you could ask questions and record his answers).

I picked up my eighty-nine-year-old aunt and she showed me where my grandmother was born. She told me lots of tales about

growing up. Being an important source of family history can enhance an elder's self image. Families should "tap" these valuable sources of information about previous generations before it is lost forever!

- Include her in family functions (a baby shower, a wedding . . .). Doug's mom came to her grandson's wedding. She wouldn't buy a new dress but, more important, she was there. (It also turned out to be the last family photo with her in it!)
- Bring visitors to see her (an old friend, a new baby, a favorite pet . . .). Days can be long with little to do.
- Bring a DVD to his residence and watch it with him.
- Give her gift certificates to get her hair done.
- Go for a pedicure or manicure together.
- If he likes cards, play with him.
- Contract with a florist to deliver flowers monthly.
- Hire a companion to take him on regular walks or drives.
- Hire a personal trainer to go to her home and work with her (several seniors we've worked with had their own trainers).
- Hire someone to come and read to him regularly (interest, companionship).
- Pick up a gift for her to give to someone else.

One day while visiting my grandmother, I asked her if she wanted anything. Her reply surprised me. She said, "See that man sweeping the floor? His wife is expecting a baby. Would you buy a baby present for me?" One Christmas, Judy made a gift to go at each person's place at the table in her grandmother's residence. Her grandmother had grown up in the family's bake shop. Judy made Christmas cake, shortbread, and gingerbread for each resident. Each was small, safe to eat, and carefully and colorfully wrapped. The gifts to the residents were from her grandmother.

- Ask for help with gift wrapping, tree decorating (people need to feel useful).
- Give a fun, frivolous conversation piece.

This week a client received a colorful doll that moved and sang, "Girls just want to have fun." Many people were dancing like teenagers and greatly enjoying the moment.

Some inexpensive but practical gifts you might consider:

- Gift certificates for taxis
- A bulletin board
- A box of homemade cookies
- Homemade jam
- A deck of cards
- Kleenex
- Favorite candy or chocolate
- Body lotion, hand lotion, shower cap
- Soap, shampoo, toothpaste
- Writing paper, envelopes and stamps, pen
- A magazine subscription
- A newspaper subscription
- Slippers
- New robe
- Lounging or track pants
- Fresh fruit
- Coasters
- A coffee mug
- A new lampshade
- Personal hygiene items
- Mad money
- Vitamins
- A mechanical bed or chair
- A vase
- A fish or a bird, if permitted (company and something to look after)
- A CD player and an audio book
- A new space-saving television
- A big-button telephone
- Batteries
- A large-print crossword book
- Room freshener
- A large, colorful bib (if needed)
- Art or craft supplies
- Frozen gourmet dinners

You can also encourage your loved one to participate in getting gifts for others. Some examples:

- "We're doing a Thanksgiving basket for a needy family. Would you like to help us choose the items?"
- "Your friends are celebrating their fiftieth anniversary. Would you like to send a card?"
- "The activity director is going to have her first baby. Do you think we could talk with the manager and plan a baby shower for her?"
- "The veterans' hospital asked for cards, notepaper, and stamps. I'll get them, but would you help wrap them?"
- "Your grandchild is fundraising for her ball team. Would you look in this catalog to see if you can see some small thing you could order? I'm sure it would mean a lot to her."
- "Your great-grandchild needs new skates. Would you like to contribute toward them?"

ENJOY YOUR TIME WITH YOUR GRANDCHILDREN!

CHAPTER 16

Boomers!
What about the Future?

AS EACH YEAR GOES BY, the need for affordable senior housing is going to increase. What can we, our children, or our grandchildren do to prepare for the future?

Many seniors are selling their homes and buying condominiums. People under sixty-five are buying large condos, while people over sixty-five are buying smaller units. They are carefully choosing their locations. Some people are planning to stay in their location for a short time, while others intend to live in their chosen home "forever." We see people investing in housing to rent out now and live in later.

Look carefully at your monthly commitments. Remember that if you are looking at a condominium, the smaller the building the larger the regular financial commitments.

"Granny suites" are growing in popularity. You can plan a home that can give you privacy, independence, and the capacity for some family members to live in the dwelling for support when needed.

Seventy-nine million baby boomers are marching into retirement and a third of them could live to be ninety-five. Will their money last? Will they be able to keep up their standard of living? Do they realize how much it costs to get old?

What support will future governments be able to offer to an aging population? Will affordable senior housing keep up with the increasing demand?

TIME TO THINK AND PLAN AHEAD!

About the Authors

DOUG AND JUDY ROBINSON retired from teaching in 1992. At that time, they downsized. As Senior Move Managers, they have been downsizing seniors since 1996. Over the years, they have shared their expertise on radio talk shows, national and local television, and through many live seminars near and far.

They have three children and nine wonderful grandchildren.

Visit their Web site at *www.seniormoves.ca.*

TO ORDER MORE COPIES, CONTACT:

General Store Publishing House
499 O'Brien Road, Box 415
Renfrew, Ontario, Canada K7V 4A6
Tel 1.800.465.6072 · Fax 1.613.432.7184
www.gsph.com